THE POETICAL WORKS OF ROBERT BURNS.

WITH A SKETCH OF THE AUTHOR'S LIFE.

IN THREE VOLUMES.

VOLUME II.

BOSTON:
LITTLE, BROWN AND COMPANY.
NEW YORK: BLAKEMAN AND MASON.
CINCINNATI: RICKEY AND CARROLL.
M.DCCC.LXIII.

RIVERSIDE, CAMBRIDGE:
STEREOTYPED AND PRINTED BY H. O. HOUGHTON

CONTENTS

OF

THE SECOND VOLUME.

*** The Italic letters indicate the publication in which the several compositions respectively appeared: see note prefixed to the Contents of Volume I.

ROBERT BURNS.

1759–1796.

THE HOLY FAIR.

"A robe of seeming truth and trust
  Hid crafty observation;
And secret hung, with poisoned crust,
  The dirk of Defamation:
A mask that like the gorget showed,
  Dye-varying on the pigeon;
And for a mantle large and broad,
  He wrapt him in Religion."

Hypocrisy à-la-Mode.

The transactions described in this piece are those which attended a rural celebration of the communion in Scotland till a very recent period, if not till the present day. But it is important to notice that the rite itself, and even the place where it was administered, form no part of the picture. Burns limits himself to the assemblage, partly composed of parishioners and partly of strangers, which takes place on such occasions, in some open space near the church, where a succession of clergymen, usually from the neighboring parishes, give from a *tent* or movable pulpit a succession of services, while a lesser body are attending the more solemn ritual within doors. That Burns's description is not exaggerated in any particular, is rendered certain by a passage which we shall take leave to adduce from a pamphlet published in the year of the poet's birth, under the title of *A Letter from a Blacksmith to the Ministers and Elders of the Church of Scotland.* "In Scotland," says this writer, "they run from kirk to kirk, and flock to see a sacrament, and make the same use of it that the papists do of their pilgrimages and processions; that is, indulge themselves in drunkenness, folly, and idleness. Most of the servants, when they agree to serve their masters in the western parts of the kingdom, make a special provision that they shall have liberty to go to a certain number of fairs, or to an equal number of sacraments; and as they consider a sacrament, or an occasion (as they call the administration of the Lord's Supper), in a neighboring parish in the same light in which they do at a fair, so they behave at it much in the same manner."

It may be added, that the *Leith Races* of Fergusson served Burns as a literary model. The Edinburgh poet is there conducted to the festive scene by an imaginary being, whom he names MIRTH, exactly as Burns is conducted to the Holy Fair by FUN; but the poetical painting of the Ayrshire bard far distances that of his predecessor.

UPON a simmer Sunday-morn,
  When Nature's face is fair,
I walkèd forth to view the corn,
  And snuff the cauler air. fresh
The rising sun o'er Galston muirs,
  Wi' glorious light was glintin'; flashing

The hares were hirplin' down the furs, limping / furrows
The lav'rocks they were chantin'
Fu' sweet that day.

As lightsomely I glowr'd abroad, looked
To see a scene sae gay,
Three hizzies, early at the road, wenches
Cam skelpin' up the way. walking along
Twa had manteeles o' dolefu' black,
But ane wi' lyart lining; gray
The third, that gaed a-wee a-back,
Was in the fashion shining,
Fu' gay that day.

The twa appeared like sisters twin,
In feature, form, and claes;
Their visage withered, lang, and thin,
And sour as ony slaes.
The third cam up, hap-step-an'-lowp,[1]
As light as ony lambie,
And wi' a curchie low did stoop,
As soon as e'er she saw me,
Fu' kind that day.

Wi' bonnet aff, quoth I: "Sweet lass,
I think ye seem to ken me;
I'm sure I've seen that bonny face,
But yet I canna name ye."

[1] Hop-skip-and-leap.

Quo' she, and laughin' as she spak,
  And taks me by the hands:
"Ye, for my sake, hae gien the feck most
  Of a' the ten commands
      A screed some day. rent

"My name is Fun — your cronie dear,
  The nearest friend ye hae;
And this is Superstition here,
  And that's Hypocrisy.
I'm gaun to Mauchline Holy Fair,
  To spend an hour in daffin': sport
Gin ye'll go there, yon runkled pair, wrinkled
  We will get famous laughin'
      At them this day."

Quoth I: "With a' my heart, I'll do't;
  I'll get my Sunday's sark on,
And meet you on the holy spot —
  Faith, we'se hae fine remarkin'!"
Then I gaed hame at crowdie-time, breakfast
  And soon I made me ready;
For roads were clad, from side to side,
  Wi' mony a weary body,
      In droves that day.

Here farmers gash, in ridin' graith, sensible — attire
  Gaed hoddin by their cotters; jogging
There, swankies young, in braw braid claith, striplings

Are springin' o'er the gutters.
The lasses, skelpin' barefit, thrang, walking along
In silks and scarlets glitter;
Wi' sweet-milk cheese, in monie a whang, cut
And farls baked wi' butter, cakes
Fu' crump that day. crisp

When by the plate we set our nose,
Weel heapèd up wi' ha'pence,
A greedy glowr Black-bonnet throws, look
And we maun draw our tippence.[1]
Then in we go to see the show;
On every side they're gath'rin',
Some carrying dails, some chairs, and stools, portions (of food)?
And some are busy blethrin' chatting
Right loud that day.

Here stands a shed to fend the showers,
And screen our country gentry,
There, Racer Jess,[2] and twa-three w——s,
Are blinkin' at the entry.
Here sits a raw of tittlin' jauds,
Wi' heaving breast and bare neck,
And there a batch o' wabster lads, weaver
Blackguarding frae Kilmarnock
For fun this day,

[1] Black-bonnet, a cant name for the elder stationed beside the plate at the door for receiving the offerings of the congregation.

[2] A poor half-witted girl of the name of Gibson (daughter of Poosie Nansie), who was remarkable for pedestrian powers, and sometimes went with messages for hire.

Here, some are thinkin' on their sins,
  And some upo' their claes;
Ane curses feet that fyl'd his shins,
  Anither sighs and prays:
On this hand sits a chosen swatch, sample
  Wi' screwed-up, grace-proud faces;
On that a set o' chaps at watch,
  Thrang winkin' on the lasses busily occupied
      To chairs that day.

Oh happy is that man and blest!
  Nae wonder that it pride him,
Wha's ain dear lass, that he likes best,
  Comes clinkin' down beside him! sitting
Wi' arm reposed on the chair back,
  He sweetly does compose him;
Which, by degrees, slips round her neck,
  An's loof upon her bosom, palm
      Unkenn'd that day.

Now a' the congregation o'er
  Is silent expectation:
For Moodie speels the holy door, climbs
  Wi' tidings o' d——tion.[1]

[1] In the Kilmarnock edition, the word was salvation; it was changed at the suggestion of Dr. Blair of Edinburgh. Moodie was the minister of Riccarton, and one of the heroes of *The Twa Herds.* He was a never-failing assistant at the Mauchline sacraments. His personal appearance and style of oratory were exactly such as described by the poet. He dwelt chiefly on the terrors of the law. On one occasion, he told the audience that they would find the text in John viii.

Should Hornie, as in ancient days
'Mang sons o' God present him,
The very sight o' Moodie's face
To's ain het hame had sent him hot
Wi' fright that day.

Hear how he clears the points o' Faith
Wi' rattlin' and wi' thumpin'!
Now meekly calm, now wild in wrath,
He's stampin' and he's jumpin'!
His lengthened chin, his turned-up snout,
His eldritch squeel and gestures, unearthly
Oh how they fire the heart devout,
Like cantharidian plasters,
On sic a day!

But hark! the tent has changed its voice;
There's peace and rest nae langer;
For a' the real judges rise,
They canna sit for anger.
Smith opens out his cauld harangues,[1]
On practice and on morals;
And aff the godly pour in thrangs,
To gie the jars and barrels
A lift that day.

44, but it was so applicable to their case, that there was no need of his reading it to them. The verse begins: "Ye are of your father the devil," etc.

1 Mr. (afterwards Dr.) George Smith, minister of Galston — the same whom the poet introduces in a different feeling, under the appellation of Irvine-side in *The Kirk's Alarm.* Burns meant on this occasion to compliment him on his

What signifies his barren shine
Of moral powers and reason?
His English style and gesture fine
Are a' clean out o' season.
Like Socrates or Antonine,
Or some auld pagan heathen,
The moral man he does define,
But ne'er a word o' faith in
That's right that day

In guid time comes an antidote
Against sic poisoned nostrum;
For Peebles, frae the Water-fit,[1]
Ascends the holy rostrum:
See, up he's got the Word o' God,
And meek and mim has viewed it, primly
While Common Sense has ta'en the road,
And aff and up the Cowgate,[2]
Fast, fast that day.

rational mode of preaching, but the friends of the divine regarded the stanza as calculated to injure his popularity.

1 The Rev. Mr. (afterwards Dr.) William Peebles, minister of Newton-upon-Ayr, often called, from its geographical situation, the *Water-fit.* He was in great favor at Ayr among the orthodox party, though much inferior in ability to the moderate ministers of that ancient burgh.

2 The Cowgate is a street running off the main one of Mauchline, exactly opposite the entrance to the church-yard. The sense of the passage might be supposed allegorical, and this is the theory which the present editor is inclined to adopt. He must, however, state that a more literal sense is attached to it by the best-informed persons in Mauchline. It is said that Mr. Mackenzie, the surgeon of the village, and a friend of Burns, had recently written on some controversial topic

Wee Miller [1] niest the guard relieves, next
And orthodoxy raibles, rattles
Though in his heart he weel believes,
And thinks it auld wives' fables:
But, faith! the birkie wants a manse, fellow
So, cannily he hums them;
Although his carnal wit and sense
Like hafflins-ways o'ercomes him half-ways
At times that day.

Now but and ben the change-house fills, throughout
Wi' yill-caup commentators; a'e-pot
Here's crying out for bakes and gills, biscuits
And there the pint-stoup clatters;
While thick and thrang, and loud and lang,
Wi' logic and wi' scripture,
They raise a din, that, in the end,
Is like to breed a rupture
O' wrath that day.

under the title of *Common Sense*. On the particular day which Burns is supposed to have had in view, Mackenzie was engaged to join Sir John Whitefoord of Ballochmyle, and go to Dumfries House, in Auchinleck parish, in order to dine with the Earl of Dumfries. The doctor, therefore, after attending church, and listening to some of the out-door harangues, was seen to leave the assembly, and go off along the Cowgate, on his way to Ballochmyle, exactly as Peebles ascended the rostrum.

[1] The Rev. Mr. Miller, afterwards minister of Kilmaurs. He was of remarkably low stature, but enormous girth. Burns believed him at the time to lean at heart to the moderate party. This stanza, virtually the most depreciatory in the whole poem, is said to have retarded Miller's advancement.

Leeze me on drink! it gies us mair Commend to
  Than either school or college:
It kindles wit, it waukens lair, learning
  It pangs us fou o' knowledge. crams
Be 't whisky gill, or penny wheep, small-beer
  Or ony stronger potion,
It never fails, on drinking deep,
  To kittle up our notion tickle
    By night or day.

The lads and lasses, blithely bent
  To mind baith saul and body,
Sit round the table weel content,
  And steer about the toddy.
On this ane's dress, and that ane's leuk,
  They're making observations;
While some are cozie i' the neuk,
  And formin' assignations
    To meet some day.

But now the L—'s ain trumpet touts,
  Till a' the hills are rairin', roaring
And echoes back return the shouts —
  Black Russell[1] is na sparin':

[1] The Rev. John Russell, at this time minister of the Chapel-of-Ease, Kilmarnock, afterwards minister of Stirling, one of the heroes of *The Twa Herds.* A correspondent says: "He was the most tremendous man I ever saw: Black Hugh Macpherson was a beauty in comparison. His voice was like thunder, and his sentiments were such as must have shocked any class of hearers in the least more refined than those whom he usually addressed."

His piercing words, like Highland swords,
  Divide the joints and marrow;
His talk o' hell, whare devils dwell,
  Our vera sauls does harrow[1]
      Wi' fright that day.

A vast, unbottomed, boundless pit,
  Filled fou o' lowin' brunstane, blazing
Wha's ragin' flame, and scorchin' heat,
  Wad melt the hardest whunstane!
The half-asleep start up wi' fear,
  And think they hear it roarin',
When presently it does appear
  'Twas but some neebor snorin',
      Asleep that day.

'Twad be owre lang a tale to tell
  How monie stories past,
And how they crowded to the yill, ale
  When they were a' dismist:
How drink gaed round, in cogs and caups, pails
  Amang the forms and benches:
And cheese and bread, frae women's laps,
  Was dealt about in lunches,
      And dauds that day. hunks

In comes a gaucy, gash guidwife, fat—talkative
  And sits down by the fire,
Syne draws her kebbuck and her knife; cheese

[1] Shakspeare's *Hamlet.* — *B.*

The lasses they are shyer.
The auld guidmen, about the grace,
Frae side to side they bother,
Till some ane by his bonnet lays,
And gies them't like a tether,
Fu' lang that day.

Waesucks! for him that gets nae lass,
Or lasses that hae naething!
Sma' need has he to say a grace,
Or melvie his braw claithing! soil with meal
Oh wives, be mindfu' ance yoursel'
How bonny lads ye wanted,
And dinna, for a kebbuck-heel, cheese-rind
Let lasses be affronted
On sic a day!

Now Clinkumbell,[1] wi' rattlin' tow,
Begins to jow and croon; peal — roar
Some swagger hame, the best they dow, can
Some wait the afternoon.
At slaps the billies halt a blink, gates
Till lasses strip their shoon:
Wi' faith and hope, and love and drink,
They're a' in famous tune
For crack that day.

How monie hearts this day converts
O' sinners and o' lasses!

1 Variation — "Now Robin Gib," etc.

Their hearts o' stane, gin night, are gane,
  As saft as ony flesh is.
There's some are fou o' love divine;
  There's some are fou o' brandy;
And monie jobs that day begin
  May end in houghmagandy
      Some ither day.

ON A SCOTCH BARD,

GONE TO THE WEST INDIES.

A' YE wha live by sowps o' drink,
A' ye wha live by crambo-clink, versifying
A' ye wha live and never think,
      Come, mourn wi' me!
Our billie's gien us a' a jink,[1]
      And owre the sea.

Lament him a' ye rantin' core,
Wha dearly like a random-splore, frolic
Nae mair he'll join the merry roar
      In social key;
For now he's ta'en anither shore,
      And owre the sea!

1 "Our brother has eluded us all."

Auld cantie Kyle may weepers wear, cheerful
And stain them wi' the saut, saut tear;
'Twill mak her poor auld heart, I fear,
In flinders flee; splinters
He was her laureate monie a year,
That's owre the sea.

He saw misfortune's cauld nor-west
Lang mustering up a bitter blast;
A jillet brak his heart at last, jilt
Ill may she be!
So, took a berth afore the mast,
And owre the sea.

To tremble under Fortune's cummock, rod
On scarce a bellyfu' o' drummock, meal and water
Wi' his proud, independent stomach,
Could ill agree;
So row't his hurdies in a hammock, rolled — loins
And owre the sea.

He ne'er was gien to great misguiding,
Yet coin his pouches wadna bide in;
Wi' him it ne'er was under hiding —
He dealt it free:
The Muse was a' that he took pride in,
That's owre the sea.

Jamaica bodies, use him weel,
And hap him in a cozie biel: wrap — snug shelter

Ye'll find him aye a dainty chiel,
And fou o' glee;
He wadna wranged the very deil,
That's owre the sea.

Fareweel, my rhyme-composing billie! comrade
Your native soil was right ill-willie;
But may ye flourish like a lily,
Now bonnilie!
I'll toast ye in my hinmost gillie, gill
Though owre the sea!

A BARD'S EPITAPH.

In a different spirit, Burns wrote an epitaph for himself — a confession of his errors so solemn and so touching, as to take the sting from every other comment on the subject.

Is there a whim-inspirèd fool,
Owre fast for thought, owre hot for rule,
Owre blate to seek, owre proud to bashful
snool, succumb
Let him draw near;
And owre this grassy heap sing dool,
And drap a tear.

Is there a bard of rustic song,
Who, noteless, steals the crowds among,
That weekly this aréa throng,
Oh, pass not by!
But, with a frater-feeling strong,
Here heave a sigh.

Is there a man, whose judgment clear,
Can others teach the course to steer,
Yet runs himself life's mad career,
Wild as the wave;
Here pause — and, through the starting tear
Survey this grave.

The poor inhabitant below,
Was quick to learn, and wise to know,
And keenly felt the friendly glow,
And softer flame;
But thoughtless follies laid him low,
And stained his name!

Reader, attend — whether thy soul
Soars fancy's flights beyond the pole,
Or darkling grubs this earthly hole,
In low pursuit;
Know, prudent, cautious self-control
Is wisdom's root.

DEDICATION TO GAVIN HAMILTON, Esq.

In dedicating his Poems to Gavin Hamilton, Burns took the opportunity not merely to characterize that generous-natured man, but to throw out a few parting sarcasms at orthodoxy and her partisans. This poem, however, was not placed at the front of the volume, though included in its pages.

Expect na, sir, in this narration,
A fleechin, fleth'rin dedication, wheedling—flattering
To roose you up, and ca' you guid, praise
And sprung o' great and noble bluid,
Because ye're surnamed like his Grace;[1]
Perhaps related to the race;
Then when I'm tired, and sae are ye,
Wi' monie a fulsome, sinfu' lie,
Set up a face, how I stop short,
For fear your modesty be hurt.

This may do—maun do, sir, wi' them wha
Maun please the great folk for a wamefou; belly-full
For me! sae laigh I needna bow,
For, L— be thankit, I can plough;
And when I downa yoke a naig, cannot
Then, L— be thankit, I can beg;

[1] The Duke of Hamilton.

Sae I shall say, and that's nae flatterin',
It's just sic poet, and sic patron.

The Poet, some guid angel help him,
Or else, I fear, some ill ane skelp him, beat
He may do weel for a' he's done yet,
But only he's no just begun yet.

The Patron (sir, ye maun forgie me,
I winna lie, come what will o' me),
On every hand it will allowed be,
He's just — nae better than he should be.

I readily and freely grant,
He downa see a poor man want; cannot
What's no his ain he winna tak it,
What ance he says he winna break it;
Ought he can lend he'll no refus't
Till aft his gudeness is abused;
And rascals whiles that do him wrang,
Even that, he does na mind it lang:
As master, landlord, husband, father,
He does na fail his part in either.

But then nae thanks to him for a' that,
Nae godly symptom ye can ca' that;
It's naething but a milder feature
Of our poor sinfu', córrupt nature:
Ye'll get the best o' moral works,
'Mang black Gentoos and pagan Turks,

Or hunters wild on Ponotaxi,
Wha never heard of orthodoxy.
That he's the poor man's friend in need,
The gentleman in word and deed,
It's no through terror of d——tion;
It's just a carnal inclination.

Morality, thou deadly bane,
Thy tens o' thousands thou hast slain!
Vain is his hope whose stay and trust is
In moral mercy, truth, and justice!

No — stretch a point to catch a plack; penny
Abuse a brother to his back;
Steal through a winnock frae a w——,
But point the rake that taks the door;
Be to the poor like ony whunstane,
And haud their noses to the grunstane;
Ply every art o' legal thieving;
No matter — stick to sound believing!

Learn three-mile prayers, and half-mile graces,
Wi' weel-spread looves, and lang wry faces; palms
Grunt up a solemn, lengthened groan,
And d— a' parties but your own;
I'll warrant, then, ye're nae deceiver —
A steady, sturdy, stanch believer.

Oh ye wha leave the springs o' Calvin,
For gumlie dubs of your ain delvin'! muddy ponds

Ye sons of heresy and error,
Ye'll some day squeel in quaking terror!
When Vengeance draws the sword in wrath,
And in the fire throws the sheath;
When Ruin, with his sweeping besom,
Just frets, till Heaven commission gies him:
While o'er the harp pale Misery moans,
And strikes the ever-deepening tones,
Still louder shrieks, and heavier groans!

Your pardon, sir, for this digression,
I maist forgot my dedication;
But when divinity comes 'cross me,
My readers still are sure to lose me.

So, sir, ye see 'twas nae daft vapour, foolish
But I maturely thought it proper,
When a' my works I did review,
To dedicate them, sir, to you:
Because (ye need na tak it ill)
I thought them something like yoursel'.

Then patronise them wi' your favour,
And your petitioner shall ever ——
I had amaist said, ever pray,
But that's a word I need na say:
For prayin' I hae little skill o't;
I'm baith dead sweer, and wretched ill o't; unwilling
But I'se repeat each poor man's prayer
That kens or hears about you, sir: —

"May ne'er Misfortune's gowling bark
Howl through the dwelling o' the Clerk![1]
May ne'er his generous, honest heart,
For that same generous spirit smart!
May Kennedy's far-honoured name
Lang beat his hymeneal flame, feed
Till Hamiltons, at least a dizzen,
Are by their canty fireside risen: cheerful
Five bonny lasses round their table,
And seven braw fellows, stout and able,
To serve their king and country weel,
By word, or pen, or pointed steel!
May health and peace, with mutual rays,
Shine on the evening o' his days,
Till his wee curlie John's ier-oe, great-grandchild
When ebbing life nae mair shall flow,
The last, sad mournful rites bestow."

I will not wind a lang conclusion
With complimentary effusion:
But whilst your wishes and endeavours
Are blest wi' fortune's smiles and favours,
I am, dear sir, with zeal most fervent,
Your much indebted, humble servant.

But if (which powers above prevent!)
That iron-hearted carl, Want,
Attended in his grim advances

[1] A sobriquet for Mr. Hamilton, probably because of his acting in this capacity to some of the county courts.

By sad mistakes and black mischances,
While hopes, and joys, and pleasures fly him,
Make you as poor a dog as I am,
Your humble servant then no more;
For who would humbly serve the poor?
But by a poor man's hopes in Heaven!
While recollection's power is given,
If, in the vale of humble life,
The victim sad of fortune's strife,
I, through the tender-gushing tear,
Should recognise my master dear,
If friendless, low, we meet together,
Then, sir, your hand — my friend and brother!

FAREWELL TO THE BRETHREN OF ST. JAMES'S LODGE, TORBOLTON.

Tune — *Good-night, and Joy be wi' you a'.*

Adieu! a heart-warm, fond adieu!
  Dear brothers of the *mystic tie!*
Ye favoured, ye *enlightened* few,
  Companions of my social joy.
Though I to foreign lands must hie,
  Pursuing Fortune's slidd'ry ba',
With melting heart, and brimful eye,
  I'll mind you still, though far awa'. remember

Oft have I met your social band,
  And spent the cheerful, festive night;
Oft, honoured with supreme command,
  Presided o'er the *Sons of Light:*
And by that *hieroglyphic* bright
  Which none but *Craftsmen* ever saw!
Strong Memory on my heart shall write
  Those happy scenes when far awa'.

May Freedom, Harmony, and Love,
  Unite you in the *grand design,*
Beneath the Omniscient Eye above,
  The glorious Architect Divine!
That you may keep the *unerring line,*
  Still rising by the *plummet's law,*
Till Order bright completely shine,
  Shall be my prayer when far awa'.

And *you,* farewell! whose merits claim,
  Justly, that *highest badge* to wear!
Heaven bless your honoured, noble name,
  To *masonry* and *Scotia* dear!
A last request permit me here,
  When yearly ye assemble a',
One *round* — I ask it with *a tear* —
  To him, *the Bard that's far awa'.*[1]

[1] The person alluded to in the last stanza was Major-General James Montgomery (a younger brother of Hugh Montgomery of Coilsfield), who now enjoyed the dignity of the Worshipful Grand Master in this village lodge, while Robert Burns was Depute Master.

ON A PROCESSION OF THE ST. JAMES'S LODGE.

The St. James's Lodge at this time met in a small stifling back-room connected with the inn of the village — a humble cottage-like place of entertainment kept by one Manson. On the approach of St. John's Day, the 24th of June, when a procession of the lodge was contemplated, Burns sent a rhymed note on the subject to his medical friend Mr. Mackenzie, with whom, it may be explained, he had lately had some controversy on the origin of morals.

FRIDAY first's the day appointed
By the Right Worshipful anointed,
  To hold our grand procession;
To get a blad o' Johnnie's morals, liberal portion
And taste a swatch o' Manson's barrels, sample
  I' the way of our profession.
The Master and the Brotherhood
  Would a' be glad to see you;
For me I would be mair than proud
  To share the mercies wi' you. entertainment
    If Death, then, wi' skaith, then, hurt
      Some mortal heart is hechtin', threatening
    Inform him, and storm him,
      That Saturday you'll fecht him. fight

ROBERT BURNS.

MOSSGIEL, *An. M.* 5790.

THE SONS OF OLD KILLIE.

TUNE — *Shawnboy.*

Burns joined on at least one occasion in the festivities of the Kilmarnock Lodge, presided over by his friend William Parker; on which occasion he produced an appropriate song.

YE sons of old Killie, assembled by Willie,
  To follow the noble vocation;
Your thrifty old mother has scarce such another
  To sit in that honourèd station.
I've little to say, but only to pray,
  As praying's the ton of your fashion;
A prayer from the Muse you well may excuse,
  'Tis seldom her favourite passion.

Ye powers who preside o'er the wind and the tide,
  Who markèd each element's border;
Who formèd this frame with beneficent aim,
  Whose sovereign statute is order;
Within this dear mansion may wayward Contention
  Or witherèd Envy ne'er enter;
May Secrecy round be the mystical bound,
  And Brotherly Love be the centre.

THE BONNIE LASS O' BALLOCHMYLE.

The beautiful estate of Ballochmyle on the Ayr, near Mauchline, had recently been transferred from the Whitefoords to Mr. Claud Alexander, a gentleman well connected in the west of Scotland, who had realized a large fortune as paymaster-general of the East India Company's troops in Bengal. He had lately come to reside at the mansion-house. The steep banks of the river at this place form a scene of natural loveliness which has few matches, and Burns loved to wander there. In an evening of early summer, Miss Wilhelmina Alexander, the sister of the new laird, walking out along the braes after dinner, encountered a plain-looking man in rustic attire, who appeared to be musing, with his shoulder leaning against a tree. According to her own account: "The grounds being forbidden to unauthorized strangers — the evening being far advanced, and the encounter very sudden — she was startled, but instantly recovered herself, and passed on." During his walk homeward Burns composed a song descriptive of the scene and the meeting.

'Twas even — the dewy fields were green,
  On every blade the pearls hang![1]
The Zephyr wantoned round the bean,
  And bore its fragrant sweets alang;

[1] *Hang*, Scotticism for *hung*.

In every glen the mavis sang,
  All nature listening seemed the while,
Except where greenwood echoes rang,
  Amang the braes o' Ballochmyle.

With careless step I onward strayed,
  My heart rejoiced in Nature's joy,
When, musing in a lonely glade,
  A maiden fair I chanced to spy.
Her look was like the morning's eye,
  Her air like Nature's vernal smile,
Perfection whispered passing by,
  Behold the lass o' Ballochmyle ![1]

Fair is the morn in flowery May,
  And sweet is night in Autumn mild,
When roving through the garden gay,
  Or wandering in the lonely wild:
But woman, Nature's darling child!
  There all her charms she does compile;
Even there her other works are foiled
  By the bonnie lass o' Ballochmyle.

Oh, had she been a country maid,
  And I the happy country swain,
Though sheltered in the lowest shed
  That ever rose on Scotland's plain,

[1] Variation—

The lily's hue and rose's dye
  Bespoke the lass o' Ballochmyle.

Through weary winter's wind and rain,
With joy, with rapture, I would toil,
And nightly to my bosom strain
The bonnie lass o' Ballochmyle.

Then pride might climb the slippery steep,
Where fame and honours lofty shine ;
And thirst of gold might tempt the deep,
Or downward seek the Indian mine ;
Give me the cot below the pine,
To tend the flocks, or till the soil,
And every day has joys divine
With the bonnie lass o' Ballochmyle.

TO MR. JOHN KENNEDY.

(Between 3d and 16th August, 1786.)

FAREWELL, dear friend ! may guid-luck hit you,
And 'mang her favourites admit you.
If e'er Detraction shore to smit you, threaten
May nane believe him,
And ony deil that thinks to get you,
Good L—, deceive him.

R. B.

THE FAREWELL.

"The valiant, in himself, what can he suffer?
Or what does he regard his single woes?
But when, alas! he multiplies himself,
To dearer selves, to the loved tender fair,
To those whose bliss, whose being hangs upon him,
To helpless children! — then, oh then! he feels
The point of misery festering in his heart,
And weakly weeps his fortune like a coward.
Such, such am I! undone!"

THOMSON'S *Edward and Eleanora.*

FAREWELL, old Scotia's bleak domains,
Far dearer than the torrid plains
Where rich ananas blow!
Farewell, a mother's blessing dear!
A brother's sigh! a sister's tear!
My Jean's heart-rending throe!
Farewell, my Bess! though thou'rt bereft
Of my parental care,
A faithful brother I have left,
My part in him thou'lt share!
Adieu too, to you too,
My Smith, my bosom frien';
When kindly you mind me, remember
Oh then befriend my Jean!

What bursting anguish tears my heart!
From thee, my Jeanie, must I part?

Thou, weeping, answ'rest "No!"
Alas! misfortune stares my face,
And points to ruin and disgrace;
I for thy sake must go!
Thee, Hamilton, and Aiken dear,
A grateful, warm adieu!
I, with a much-indebted tear,
Shall still remember you!
All-hail then, the gale then,
Wafts me from thee, dear shore!
It rustles, and whistles —
I'll never see thee more!

LINES WRITTEN ON A BANK-NOTE.[1]

WAE worth thy power, thou cursed leaf,
Fell source o' a' my wo and grief:
For lack o' thee I've lost my lass,
For lack o' thee I scrimp my glass;
I see the children of affliction
Unaided, through thy cursed restriction.
I've seen the oppressor's cruel smile
Amid his hapless victim's spoil,

[1] "The above verses, in the handwriting of Burns, are copied from a bank-note, in the possession of Mr. James F. Gracie of Dumfries. The note is of the Bank of Scotland, and is dated so far back as 1st March, 1780." — MOTHERWELL.

And, for thy potence, vainly wished
To crush the villain in the dust.
For lack o' thee I leave this much-loved shore,
Never perhaps to greet old Scotland more.

R. B.—Kyle.

WRITTEN

ON A BLANK LEAF OF A COPY OF THE POEMS, PRESENTED TO AN OLD SWEETHEART,[1] THEN MARRIED.

ONCE fondly loved, and still remembered dear,
  Sweet early object of my youthful vows!
Accept this mark of friendship, warm, sincere—
  Friendship! 'tis all cold duty now allows.

And when you read the simple artless rhymes,
  One friendly sigh for him—he asks no more,
Who distant burns in flaming torrid climes,
  Or haply lies beneath the Atlantic's roar.

[1] According to Dr. Currie, this old sweetheart was a girl whom the poet had seen at Kirkoswald, when he was attending school there. If so, she was a Mrs. Neilson, living in Ayr.

VERSES WRITTEN UNDER VIOLENT GRIEF.[1]

Accept the gift a friend sincere
 Wad on thy worth be pressin';
Remembrance oft may start a tear,
But oh! that tenderness forbear,
 Though 'twad my sorrows lessen.

My morning raise sae clear and fair,
 I thought sair storms wad never
Bedew the scene; but grief and care
In wildest fury hae made bare
 My peace, my hope, for ever!

You think I'm glad; oh, I pay weel
 For a' the joy I borrow,
In solitude — then, then I feel
I canna to mysel' conceal
 My deeply-ranklin' sorrow.

Farewell! within thy bosom free
 A sigh may whiles awaken;
A tear may wet thy laughin' e'e,
For Scotia's son — ance gay like thee —
 Now hopeless, comfortless, forsaken!

[1] These verses were probably written, like the preceding, on a copy of the volume of poems. They were first published in the *Sun* newspaper, April, 1823.

THE CALF.

TO THE REV. MR. JAMES STEVEN,[1]

On his Text, *Malachi*, iv. 2. — "And ye shall go forth, and grow up as CALVES of the stall."

RIGHT, sir! your text I'll prove it true,
  Though heretics may laugh;
For instance, there's yoursel' just now,
  God knows, an unco calf!

And should some patron be so kind,
  As bless you wi' a kirk,
I doubt na, sir, but then we'll find
  Ye're still as great a stirk. year-old bullock

1 Afterwards minister of one of the Scotch churches in London, and ultimately of Kilwinning, in Ayrshire. The tradition in the family of Mr. Gavin Hamilton is, that the poet, in passing to the church at Mauchline, called at Mr. Hamilton's, who, being confined with the gout, could not accompany him, but desired him, as parents do with children, to bring home a note of the text. At the conclusion of the service, Burns called again, and sitting down for a minute at Mr. Hamilton's business-table, scribbled these verses, by way of a compliance with the request. From a memorandum by Burns himself, it would appear that there was also a wager with Mr. Hamilton as to his producing a poem in a certain time, and that he gained it by inditing *The Calf.*

But if the lover's raptured hour
  Shall ever be your lot,
Forbid it, every heavenly power,
  You e'er should be a stot! ox

Though, when some kind, connubial dear,
  Your but-and-ben adorns, kitchen and parlor
The like has been that you may wear
  A noble head of horns.

And in your lug, most reverend James, ear
  To hear you roar and rowte, bellow
Few men o' sense will doubt your claims
  To rank amang the nowte. cattle

And when ye're numbered wi' the dead,
  Below a grassy hillock,
Wi' justice they may mark your head—
  "Here lies a famous bullock!"

WILLIE CHALMERS.

Mr. William Chalmers, writer in Ayr, who had drawn up an assignation of the bard's property, was in love, and it occurred to him to ask Burns to address the admired object in his behalf. The poet, who had seen the lady, but was scarcely acquainted with her, readily complied by producing the following specimen of vicarious courtship.

WI' braw new branks in mickle pride, bridle
And eke a braw new brechan, collar
My Pegasus I'm got astride,
And up Parnassus pechin'; panting
Whiles owre a bush wi' downward crush,
The doited beastie stammers; stupid
Then up he gets, and off he sets,
For sake o' Willie Chalmers.

I doubt na, lass, that weel-kenned name
May cost a pair o' blushes;
I am nae stranger to your fame,
Nor his warm urgèd wishes.
Your bonny face sae mild and sweet,
His honest heart enamours,
And faith ye'll no be lost a whit,
Though waired on Willie Chalmers. spent

Auld Truth hersel' might swear ye're fair,
And Honour safely back her,
And Modesty assume your air,
And ne'er a ane mistak' her:
And sic twa love-inspiring een
Might fire even holy palmers;
Nae wonder, then, they've fatal been
To honest Willie Chalmers.

I doubt na fortune may you shore promise
  Some mim-mou'd pouthered priestie, prim
Fu' lifted up wi' Hebrew lore,
  And band upon his breastie:
But oh! what signifies to you
  His lexicons and grammars;
The feeling heart's the royal blue,
  And that's wi' Willie Chalmers.

Some gapin' glowrin' country laird staring
  May warsle for your favour; wrestle
May claw his lug, and straik his beard, ear
  And hoast up some palaver. cough
My bonny maid, before ye wed
  Sic clumsy-witted hammers,
Seek Heaven for help, and barefit skelp fly
  Awa' wi' Willie Chalmers.

Forgive the Bard! my fond regard
  For ane that shares my bosom,
Inspires my Muse to gie'm his dues,
  For deil a hair I roose him. flatter
May powers aboon unite you soon,
  And fructify your amours,
And every year come in mair dear
  To you and Willie Chalmers.

TAM SAMSON'S ELEGY.[1]

"An honest man's the noblest work of God." — POPE.

HAS auld Kilmarnock seen the deil?
Or great M'Kinlay[2] thrawn his heel?
Or Robertson[3] again grown weel
To preach and read?[4]
"Na, waur than a'!" cries ilka chiel —
Tam Samson's dead!

Kilmarnock lang may grunt and grane,
And sigh, and sob, and greet her lane, alone
And cleed her bairns, man, wife, and wean, clothe
In mourning weed;
To Death she's dearly paid the kane — tribute
Tam Samson's dead!

The brethren o' the mystic level
May hing their head in woefu' bevel, crook

1 Thomas Samson was one of the poet's Kilmarnock friends — a nursery and seedsman of good credit, a zealous sportsman, and a good fellow.

2 A preacher, a great favourite with the million. See *The Ordination*, stanza ii. — *B.*

3 Another preacher, an equal favourite with the few, who was at that time ailing. For him also see *The Ordination*, stanza ix. — *B.*

4 For a minister to read his sermons, as is often done by those of moderate denomination, is often a cause of great unpopularity in Scotland.

While by their nose the tears will revel,
Like ony bead;
Death's gien the lodge an unco devel — blow
Tam Samson's dead!

When Winter muffles up his cloak,
And binds the mire like a rock;
When to the loch the curlers [1] flock,
Wi' gleesome speed,
Wha will they station at the cock? — mark
Tam Samson's dead!

He was the king o' a' the core,
To guard, or draw,[2] or wick a bore,[3]
Or up the rink like Jehu roar proper line
In time o' need;
But now he lags on Death's hog-score [4] —
Tam Samson's dead!

Now safe the stately sawmont sail, salmon
And trouts be-dropped wi' crimson hail,
And eels weel kenned for souple tail,

[1] *Curling* is a game played on the ice with large round stones. The object of the player is to lay his stone as near the mark as possible, to guard that of his partner, if well laid before, and to strike off that of his antagonist; and the great art in the game is to make the stones bend in towards the mark, when it is so blocked up that they cannot be directed in a straight line. — See Jamieson's *Dict.*

[2] Go straight to the mark.

[3] Strike a stone in an oblique direction.

[4] The *hog-score* is a line crossing the course (*rink*), near its extremity: a stone which does not pass it is set aside.

And geds for greed, *pikes*
Since dark in Death's fish-creel we wail *basket*
Tam Samson dead!

Rejoice, ye birring paitricks a'; *whirring partridges*
Ye cootie moorcocks crously craw; *feather-legged*
Ye maukins, cock your fud fu' braw, *hares — tail*
Withouten dread;
Your mortal fae is now awa' —
Tam Samson's dead!

That woefu' morn be ever mourned
Saw him in shootin' graith adorned, *dress*
While pointers round impatient burned,
Frae couples freed;
But, och! he gaed, and ne'er returned! —
Tam Samson's dead!

In vain auld age his body batters;
In vain the gout his ankles fetters;
In vain the burns cam' down like waters
An acre braid!
Now every auld wife, greetin', clatters *weeping*
Tam Samson's dead!

Owre many a weary hag he limpit, *break in a moss*
And aye the tither shot he thumpit,
Till coward Death behind him jumpit,
Wi' deadly feide; *feud*
Now he proclaims, wi' tout o' trumpet,
Tam Samson's dead!

When at his heart he felt the dagger,
He reeled his wonted bottle-swagger,
But yet he drew the mortal trigger
Wi' weel-aimed heed;
"L—, five!" he cried, and owre did stagger—
Tam Samson's dead!

Ilk hoary hunter mourned a brither;
Ilk sportsman youth bemoaned a father;
Yon auld gray stane, amang the heather,
Marks out his head,
Where Burns has wrote, in rhyming blether, nonsense
Tam Samson's dead!

There low he lies, in lasting rest;
Perhaps upon his mouldering breast
Some spitefu' muirfowl bigs her nest,
To hatch and breed;
Alas! nae mair he'll them molest!—
Tam Samson's dead!

When August winds the heather wave,
And sportsmen wander by yon grave,
Three volleys let his memory crave
O' pouther and lead,
Till Echo answer frae her cave,
Tam Samson's dead!

Heaven rest his saul, where'er he be!
Is th' wish o' monie mae than me;

He had twa fauts, or maybe three,
Yet what remead? help
Ae social, honest man want we:
Tam Samson's dead!

EPITAPH.

Tam Samson's weel-worn clay here lies,
Ye canting zealots spare him;
If honest worth in heaven rise,
Ye'll mend or ye win near him. get

PER CONTRA.

Go, Fame, and canter like a fillie
Through a' the streets and neuks o' Killie;[1]
Tell every social, honest billie fellow
To cease his grievin',
For yet, unskaithed by Death's gleg sharp
gullie, knife
Tam Samson's leevin'![2]

[1] Killie is a phrase the country-folks sometimes use for Kilmarnock. — *B.*

[2] When this worthy old sportsman went out last muirfowl season, he supposed it was to be, in Ossian's phrase, "the last of his fields," and expressed an ardent wish to die and be buried in the muirs. On this hint the author composed his elegy and epitaph. — *B.*

"The following anecdote was communicated by an intimate friend of Burns, the late William Parker, Esq., of Assloss, a gentleman whose excellent social qualities, and kind, hospitable disposition, will be long remembered in Ayrshire: —

"At a jovial meeting one evening in Kilmarnock, at which Burns, Mr. Parker, and Mr. Samson were present, the poet, after the glass had circulated pretty freely, said 'He had indited a few lines, which, with the company's permission, he would read to them.' The proposal was joyfully acceded to, and the poet immediately read aloud his inimitable *Tam Samson's Elegy* —

'Has auld Kilmarnock seen the deil?' etc.

The company was convulsed with laughter, with the exception of one individual — the subject, *videlicet*, of the verses. As the burden, 'Tam Samson's dead,' came round, Tam twisted and turned his body into all variety of postures, evidently not on a bed of roses. Burns saw the bait had taken, and fixing his keen black eye on his victim (Sir Walter Scott says that Burns had the finest eyes in his head he had ever seen in mortal,) mercilessly pursued his sport with waggish glee. At last flesh and blood could stand it no longer. Tam, evidently anything but pleased, roared out vociferously: 'Ou ay, but I'm no deid yet!' Shouts of laughter followed from the rest, and Burns continued to read, ever and anon interrupted with Tam's 'Ay, but I'm no deid yet!' After he had finished, Burns took an opportunity of slipping out quietly, and returned in a few minutes with his well-known

'PER CONTRA.

Go, Fame, and canter like a fillie
Through a' the streets and neuks o' Killie;
Tell every social, honest billie
To cease his grievin',
For yet, unskaithed by Death's gleg gullie,
Tam Samson's leevin'.'

We need not say that Tam was propitiated. Like the 'humble auld beggar,' in our humorous old Scotch ballad, 'He helpit to drink his ain dregie,' and the night was spent in the usual joyous manner where Burns was the presiding genius. — MERCATOR." (*From a Glasgow newspaper*, *Dec.* 7, 1850.)

TO MR. M'ADAM OF CRAIGENGILLAN.

Among men of some figure who took notice of Burns, in consequence of the publication of his first volume of Poems was Mr. M'Adam of Craigengillan.

SIR, o'er a gill I gat your card,
  I trow it made me proud;
"See wha taks notice o' the Bard!"
  I lap and cried fu' loud.

Now diel-ma-care about their jaw,
  The senseless, gawky million:
I'll cock my nose aboon them a'—
  I'm roosed by Craigengillan! praised

'Twas noble, sir; 'twas like yoursel'
  To grant your high protection:
A great man's smile, ye ken fu' well,
  Is aye a blest infection;—

Though, by his[1] banes who in a tub
  Matched Macedonian Sandy!
On my ain legs, through dirt and dub, puddle
  I independent stand aye.

[1] Diogenes.

And when those legs to guid warm kail,
  Wi' welcome canna bear me,
A lee dike-side, a sybow-tail, lonely — wall — leek
  And barley-scone, shall cheer me. cake

Heaven spare you lang to kiss the breath
  O' many flowery simmers!
And bless your bonny lasses baith —
  I'm tauld they're lo'esome kimmers! girls.

And God bless young Dunaskin's laird,
  The blossom of our gentry,
And may he wear an auld man's beard,
  A credit to his country!

LYING AT A FRIEND'S HOUSE ONE NIGHT, THE AUTHOR LEFT THE FOLLOWING

VERSES

IN THE ROOM WHERE HE SLEPT.

Another person of local eminence whose friendly regard Burns obtained through the merit of his poetical volume, was the Rev. Mr. George Lawrie, minister of the parish of Loudon, a few miles from Mossgiel. This appears to have been a remarkably fine specimen of the old moderate clergy of the Scottish establishment — sensible, upright, kind-hearted, and with no mean taste in literature.

At Loudon manse, in a beautiful situation on Irvine

Water, entitled St. Margaret's Hill, the rustic bard paid the good minister a visit. He was received with the greatest cordiality, and immediately found himself in the midst of what was to him a scene equally novel and charming. Among the liberalities of Mr. Lawrie was a love of dancing, with a conviction that it was useful in promoting health and cheerfulness in his house. Scarcely a day passed in the manse when this exercise was not indulged. It was, therefore, exactly what might have been expected, that after dinner, or in the course of the evening, there was a dance, led by the excellent pastor and his lady, and in which Burns and other guests joined. Burns, it may be observed, though somewhat heavy-limbed, was a good dancer. He retired for the night, with feelings deeply touched by the simple refinement, good-nature, and mutual affection of this family, as well as by the unaffected kindness which had been shown to himself.

Oh thou dread Power who reign'st above,
  I know thou wilt me hear,
When for this scene of peace and love
  I make my prayer sincere!

The hoary sire — the mortal stroke,
  Long, long be pleased to spare,
To bless his filial little flock,
  And shew what good men are.

She, who her lovely offspring eyes
  With tender hopes and fears,

Oh bless her with a mother's joys,
  But spare a mother's tears!

Their hope, their stay, their darling youth,
  In manhood's dawning blush —
Bless him, thou God of love and truth,
  Up to a parent's wish!

The beauteous, seraph sister-band,
  With earnest tears I pray,
Thou know'st the snares on every hand —
  Guide thou their steps alway.

When soon or late they reach that coast,
  O'er life's rough ocean driven,
May they rejoice, no wanderer lost —
  A family in heaven! [1]

[1] Miss Louisa Lawrie possessed a scrap of verse in the poet's handwriting — a mere trifle, but apparently intended as part of a lyric description of the manse festivities. Some little license must be granted to the poet with respect to his lengthening the domestic dance so far into the night.

The night was still, and o'er the hill
  The moon shone on the castle wa';
The mavis sang, while dew-drops hang
  Around her, on the castle wa'.

Sae merrily they danced the ring,
  Frae eenin' till the cock did craw;
And aye the o'erword o' the spring, burden — tune
  Was Irvine's bairns are bonny a'.

THE GLOOMY NIGHT IS GATHERING FAST.

TUNE — *Roslin Castle.*

The time for parting came (see the preceding piece), and the benevolent host was left by Burns under feelings deeply affected by the consideration that so bright a genius should be contemplating a destiny so dismal as a clerkship in the West Indies. A wide stretch of moor had to be passed by Burns on his way home.[1] "His mind was strongly affected by parting forever with a scene where he had tasted so much elegant and social pleasure, and depressed by the contrasted gloom of his prospects. The aspect of nature harmonized with his feelings. It was a lowering and heavy evening in the end [beginning?] of autumn. The wind was up, and whistled through the rushes and long spear-grass which bent before it. The clouds were driving across the sky; and cold pelting showers at intervals added discomfort of body to cheerlessness of mind." Under these circumstances, and in this frame, Burns composed what he considered as "the last song he should ever measure in Caledonia."

THE gloomy night is gathering fast,
Loud roars the wild inconstant blast;
Yon murky cloud is foul with rain,
I see it driving o'er the plain.

[1] Professor Walker gives the ensuing narration from the conversation of Burns in Edinburgh.

The hunter now has left the moor,
The scattered coveys meet secure;
While here I wander, pressed with care,
Along the lonely banks of Ayr.

The Autumn mourns her ripening corn,
By early Winter's ravage torn;
Across her placid, azure sky,
She sees the scowling tempest fly;
Chill runs my blood to hear it rave—
I think upon the stormy wave,
Where many a danger I must dare,
Far from the bonny banks of Ayr.

'Tis not the surging billow's roar,
'Tis not that fatal deadly shore;
Though death in every shape appear,
The wretched have no more to fear!
But round my heart the ties are bound,
That heart transpierced with many a wound;
These bleed afresh, those ties I tear,
To leave the bonny banks of Ayr.

Farewell old Coila's hills and dales,
Her heathy moors and winding vales;
The scenes where wretched fancy roves,
Pursuing past, unhappy loves!
Farewell, my friends! farewell, my foes!
My peace with these, my love with those:
The bursting tears my heart declare;
Farewell the bonny banks of Ayr!

THE BRIGS OF AYR.

INSCRIBED TO JOHN BALLANTYNE, ESQ., AYR.

It seems to have been at the close of autumn that Burns composed his amusing poem, *The Brigs of Ayr*, the model of which he found in Fergusson's *Dialogue between the Plainstanes and Causeway*, though, as usual, he made an immense advance upon his predecessor. A new bridge was now building across the river at Ayr, in order to supersede an ancient structure which had long been inconvenient, and was now infirm, and as this work was proceeding under the chief magistracy of his kind patron, Mr. Ballantyne, Burns seized the occasion to make a return of gratitude by inscribing the poem to him.

THE simple Bard, rough at the rustic plough,
Learning his tuneful trade from every bough;
The chanting linnet, or the mellow thrush,
Hailing the setting sun, sweet, in the green
thorn-bush;
The soaring lark, the perching redbreast shrill,
Or deep-toned plovers, gray, wild-whistling o'er
the hill;
Shall he, nurst in the peasant's lowly shed,
To hardy independence bravely bred,
By early poverty to hardship steeled,
And trained to arms in stern misfortune's field —

Shall he be guilty of their hireling crimes,
The servile, mercenary Swiss of rhymes?
Or labour hard the panegyric close,
With all the venal soul of dedicating prose?
No! though his artless strains he rudely sings,
And throws his hand uncouthly o'er the strings,
He glows with all the spirit of the Bard,
Fame, honest Fame, his great, his dear reward!
Still, if some patron's generous care he trace,
Skilled in the secret to bestow with grace,
When Ballantyne befriends his humble name,
And hands the rustic stranger up to Fame,
With heartfelt throes his grateful bosom swells,
The godlike bliss, to give, alone excels.

'Twas when the stacks get on their winter hap, covering
And thack and rape secure the toil-won crap; thatch—rope crop
Potato bings are snuggèd up frae skaith heaps danger
Of coming Winter's biting, frosty breath;
The bees, rejoicing o'er their summer toils,
Unnumbered buds' and flowers' delicious spoils
Sealed up with frugal care in massive waxen piles,
Are doomed by man, that tyrant o'er the weak,
The death o' devils smoored wi' brimstone reek: smothered
The thundering guns are heard on every side,

The wounded coveys, reeling, scatter wide;
The feathered field-mates, bound by Nature's tie,
Sires, mothers, children, in one carnage lie;
(What warm, poetic heart, but inly bleeds,
And execrates man's savage, ruthless deeds
Nae mair the flower in field or meadow springs;
Nae mair the grove with airy concert rings,
Except, perhaps, the robin's whistling glee,
Proud o' the height o' some bit half-lang tree;
The hoary morns precede the sunny days,
Mild, calm, serene, wide spreads the noontide blaze,
While thick the gossamour waves wanton in the rays.

'Twas in that season, when a simple Bard,
Unknown and poor, Simplicity's reward,
Ae night, within the ancient brugh of Ayr, burgh
By whim inspired, or haply prest wi' care,
He left his bed, and took his wayward route,
And down by Simpson's[1] wheeled the left-about:
(Whether impelled by all-directing Fate,
To witness what I after shall narrate;[2]
Or whether, rapt in meditation high,
He wandered out he knew not where or why.)

[1] A noted tavern at the Auld Brig end. — *B.*

[2] In a MS. copy, here occur two lines omitted in print:

"Or penitential pangs for former sins
Led him to rove by quondam Merran Din's."

The drowsy Dungeon-clock[1] had numbered two,
And Wallace Tower[2] had sworn the fact was true;
The tide-swoln Firth, with sullen sounding roar,
Through the still night dashed hoarse along the shore.
All else was hushed as Nature's closed e'e;
The silent moon shone high o'er tower and tree;
The chilly frost, beneath the silver beam,
Crept, gently-crusting, o'er the glittering stream; —
When lo! on either hand the listening Bard,
The clanging sugh of whistling wings is rustle heard;
Two dusky forms dart through the midnight air,
Swift as the gos[3] drives on the wheeling hare.

Ane on the Auld Brig his airy shape uprears,
The ither flutters o'er the rising piers:
Our warlock Rhymer instantly descried
The Sprites that owre the Brigs of Ayr preside.
(That Bards are second-sighted is nae joke,
And ken the lingo of the sp'ritual folk;
Fays, Spunkies, Kelpies, a', they can explain them,

[1] A clock in a steeple connected with the old jail of Ayr. This steeple and its clock were removed some years ago.

[2] The clock in the Wallace Tower — an anomalous piece of antique masonry, surmounted by a spire, which stood in the High Street of Ayr. It was removed some years ago, and replaced by a more elegant tower, which bears its name.

[3] The gos-hawk, or falcon. — *B.*

And even the very deils they brawly ken well know
them.)
Auld Brig appeared of ancient Pictish race,
The very wrinkles Gothic in his face:
He seemed as he wi' Time had warstl'd wrestled
lang,
Yet, teughly doure, he bade toughly stout — endured
an unco bang. a severe stroke
New Brig was buskit in a braw new coat dressed
That he at Lon'on, frae ane Adams, got;
In's hand five taper staves as smooth's a bead,
Wi' virls and whirlygigums[1] at the head.
The Goth was stalking round with anxious
search,
Spying the time-worn flaws in every arch;
It chanced his new-come neebor took his e'e,
And e'en a vexed and angry heart had he!
Wi' thieveless sneer to see his modish mien, cold, dry
He, down the water, gies him this guid-e'en: —

AULD BRIG.

I doubt na, frien' ye'll think ye're nae sheep-
shank, small affair
Ance ye were streekit o'er frae bank to stretched
bank,
But gin ye be a brig as auld as me — if
Though, faith, that day I doubt ye'll never see —
There'll be, if that date come, I'll wad a bet a
boddle, doit
Some fewer whigmaleeries in your noddle. crotchets

[1] Rings and useless ornaments.

NEW BRIG.

Auld Vandal, ye but shew your little mense, civility
Just much about it wi' your scanty sense.
Will your poor, narrow footpath of a street—
Whare twa wheel-barrows tremble when they meet—
Your ruined, formless bulk o' stane and lime,
Compare wi' bonny brigs o' modern time?
There's men o' taste would tak the Ducat Stream,[1]
Though they should cast the very sark and swim, shirt
Ere they would grate their feelings wi' the view
Of sic an ugly Gothic hulk as you.

AULD BRIG.

Conceited gowk, puffed up wi' windy pride! fool
This monie a year I've stood the flood and tide;
And though wi' crazy eild I'm sair forfairn, age enfeebled
I'll be a Brig when ye're a shapeless cairn! heap of stones
As yet ye little ken about the matter,
But twa-three winters will inform ye better.
When heavy, dark, continued, a'-day rains,
Wi' deepening deluges o'erflow the plains;

[1] A noted ford just above the Auld Brig.—*B.*

When from the hills where springs the brawling Coil,
Or stately Lugar's mossy fountains boil,
Or where the Greenock winds his moorland course,
Or haunted Garpal[1] draws his feeble source,
Aroused by blustering winds and spotting thowes, thaws
In monie a torrent down his snaw-broo rowes;[2]
While crashing ice, borne on the roaring speat, flood
Sweeps dams, and mills, and brigs, a' to the gate; way
And from Glenbuck[3] down to the Ratton-key[4]
Auld Ayr is just one lengthened tumbling sea —
Then down ye'll hurl, deil nor ye never rise!
And dash the gumlie jaups up to the pouring skies: muddy waves
A lesson sadly teaching, to your cost,
That Architecture's noble art is lost!

NEW BRIG.

Fine Architecture, trowth, I needs must say't o't!

[1] The banks of Garpal Water is one of the few places in the west of Scotland where those fancy-scaring beings, known by the name of ghaists, still continue pertinaciously to inhabit. — *B.*

[2] (Snow-broth) melting snow-rolls.

[3] The source of the river Ayr. — *B.*

[4] A small landing-place above the large key. — *B.*

The L— be thankit that we've tint the gate o't! lost way
Gaunt, ghastly, ghaist-alluring edifices,
Hanging with threatening jut, like precipices;
O'erarching, mouldy, gloom-inspiring coves,
Supporting roofs fantastic, stony groves:
Windows, and doors in nameless sculpture drest,
With order, symmetry, or taste unblest;
Forms like some bedlam statuary's dream,
The crazed creations of misguided whim;
Forms might be worshipped on the bended knee,
And still the second dread command be free,
Their likeness is not found on earth, in air, or sea.
Mansions that would disgrace the building taste
Of any mason reptile, bird or beast;
Fit only for a doited monkish race, doting
Or frosty maids forsworn the dear embrace;
Or cuifs of latter times, wha held the notion fools
That sullen gloom was sterling true devotion;
Fancies that our good Brugh denies protection![1]
And soon may they expire, unblest with resurrection!

AULD BRIG.

Oh ye, my dear remembered ancient yealings, coevals

[1] An allusion to the moderatism of the Ayr clergy.

Were ye but here to share my wounded feelings!
Ye worthy Proveses, and monie a Bailie,
Wha in the paths o' righteousness did toil aye;
Ye dainty Deacons and ye douce Conveeners, grave
To whom our moderns are but causey-cleaners;
Ye godly Councils wha hae blest this town;
Ye godly brethren o' the sacred gown,
Wha meekly ga'e your hurdies to the smiters;
And (what would now be strange)[1] ye godly writers;
A' ye douce folk I've borne aboon the broo, water
Were ye but here, what would ye say or do!
How would your spirits groan in deep vexation,
To see each melancholy alteration;
And agonising, curse the time and place
When ye begat the base degenerate race!
Nae langer reverend men, their country's glory,
In plain braid Scots hold forth a plain braid story!
Nae langer thrifty citizens and douce,
Meet owre a pint, or in the council-house;
But staumrel, corky-headed, graceless half-witted gentry,
The herryment and ruin of the country; plunder
Men three parts made by tailors and by barbers,
Wha waste your weel-hained gear on well-saved d—— new brigs and harbours!

[1] A sly hint at the easy professions of the Ayr *writers* or lawyers now known to Burns.

NEW BRIG.

Now haud you there, for faith you've said enough,
And muckle mair than ye can mak to through.[1] — make good
As for your Priesthood I shall say but little,
Corbies and Clergy are a shot right kittle: — ticklish
But, under favour o' your langer beard,
Abuse o' magistrates might weel be spared.
To liken them to your auld-warld squad,
I must needs say comparisons are odd.
In Ayr, wag-wits nae mair can hae a handle
To mouth "a citizen," a term o' scandal;
Nae mair the Council waddles down the street,
In all the pomp of ignorant conceit.[2]
Men wha grew wise priggin' owre hops and raisins, — haggling
Or gathered liberal views in bonds and seisins;
If haply Knowledge, on a random tramp,
Had shored them with a glimmer of his lamp, — offered

1 Inserted in MS. copy:

"That's aye a string auld doited Graybeards harp on,
A topic for their peevishness to carp on."

2 Variation in MS.:

"Nae mair down street the Council quorum waddles,
With wigs like mainsails on their logger noddles;
No difference but bulkiest or tallest,
With comfortable dulness in for ballast:
Nor shoals nor currents need a pilot's caution,
For regularly slow, they only witness motion."

And would to Common-sense for once betrayed
them,
Plain, dull Stupidity stept kindly in to aid them.

What further clish-ma-claver might been said, palaver
What bloody wars, if sprites had blood to shed,
No man can tell; but all before their sight,
A fairy train appeared in order bright;
Adown the glittering stream they featly danced;
Bright to the moon their various dresses glanced;
They footed o'er the watery glass so neat,
The infant ice scarce bent beneath their feet;
While arts of minstrelsy among them rung,
And soul-ennobling bards heroic ditties sung.
Oh had M'Lachlan,[1] thairm-inspiring sage, cat-gut
Been there to hear this heavenly band engage,
When through his dear strathspeys they bore with Highland rage;
Or when they struck old Scotia's melting airs,
The lover's raptured joys or bleeding cares;
How would his Highland lug been nobler fired, ear

[1] A well-known performer of Scottish music on the violin. —*B.* James M'Lachlan, a Highlander, had been once footman to Lord John Campbell at Inverary. He came to Ayrshire in a fencible regiment, and was patronized by Hugh Montgomery of Coilsfield (afterwards Earl of Eglintoune), who was himself both a player and a composer.

And even his matchless hand with finer touch inspired!
No guess could tell what instrument appeared,
But all the soul of Music's self was heard;
Harmonious concert rung in every part,
While simple melody poured moving on the heart.

The Genius of the stream in front appears,
A venerable chief advanced in years;
His hoary head with water-lilies crowned,
His manly leg with garter tangle bound.
Next came the loveliest pair in all the ring,
Sweet Female Beauty hand in hand with Spring;
Then, crowned with flowery hay, came Rural Joy,
And Summer, with his fervid-beaming eye;
All-cheering Plenty, with her flowing horn,
Led yellow Autumn, wreathed with nodding corn;
Then Winter's time-bleached locks did hoary show,
By Hospitality with cloudless brow;
Next followed Courage, with his martial stride,
From where the Feal wild woody coverts hide; [1]
Benevolence, with mild, benignant air,

[1] We have here a compliment to Montgomery of Coilsfield—Soger Hugh—alluded to in the preceding note. Coilsfield is situated on the Feal, or Faile, a tributary of the Ayr.

A female form, came from the towers of Stair;[1]
Learning and Worth in equal measures trode
From simple Catrine, their long-loved abode:[2]
Last, white-robed Peace, crowned with a hazel wreath,
To rustic Agriculture did bequeath
The broken iron instruments of death;
At sight of whom our Sprites forgat their kindling wrath.

LINES ON MEETING WITH BASIL, LORD DAER.

Professor Dugald Stewart, the elegant expositor of the Scottish system of metaphysics, resided at this time in a villa at Catrine, on the Ayr, a few miles from the bard's farm. He had been made acquainted with the extraordinary productions of Burns by Mr. Mackenzie, the clever, liberal-minded surgeon of Mauchline. At the request of the professor, Mackenzie came to dinner at Catrine, accompanied by the poet. Burns was sufficiently embarrassed at the idea of meeting in the flesh a distinguished member of the literary circle of Edinburgh; but, to increase the feeling, there chanced also to be present a young scion of nobility — Lord Daer, son of the Earl of Selkirk — a positively alarming idea to the rustic

[1] A compliment to his early patroness, Mrs. Stewart of Stair. See note to *Epistle to Davie*, vol. i. p. 63.

[2] A compliment to Professor Dugald Stewart.

bard, who had as yet seen nobility no nearer than on the Ayr race-course, or whirling along the road in carriages. Lord Daer, who had been a pupil of Professor Stewart, had called, it appears, by chance. Of the meeting, Burns and Stewart have left their respective records.

THIS wot ye all whom it concerns,
I, Rhymer Robin, alias Burns,
October twenty-third,
A ne'er-to-be-forgotten day,
Sae far I sprachled up the brae, clambered
I dinner'd wi' a Lord.

I've been at drucken writers' feasts,
Nay, been bitch-fou 'mang godly priests,
Wi' reverence be it spoken;
I've even joined the honoured jorum,
When mighty squireships of the quorum
Their hydra drouth did sloken.

But wi' a Lord! — stand out my shin,
A Lord — a Peer — an Earl's son!
Up higher yet my bonnet!
And sic a Lord! — lang Scotch ells twa,
Our Peerage he o'erlooks them a',
As I look o'er my sonnet.

But oh for Hogarth's magic power!
To shew Sir Bardie's willyart glower, bewildered stare
And how he stared and stammer'd,

When goavan, as if led wi' branks, — *moving stupidly; rude bridle*
And stumpin' on his ploughman shanks,
He in the parlour hammer'd.

I sidling sheltered in a nook,
And at his Lordship steal't a look,
Like some portentous omen ;
Except good sense and social glee,
And (what surprised me) modesty,
I markèd nought uncommon.

I watched the symptoms o' the great,
The gentle pride, the lordly state,
The arrogant assuming;
The fient a pride, nae pride had he, — *devil-a-bit*
Nor sauce, nor state, that I could see,
Mair than an honest ploughman.

Then from his lordship I shall learn
Henceforth to meet with unconcern
One rank as weel's anither;
Nae honest worthy man need care
To meet with noble youthful Daer,
For he but meets a brother.[1]

[1] Lord Daer was a young nobleman of the greatest promise. He had just returned from France, where he cultivated the society of some of those men who afterwards figured in the Revolution (particularly Condorcet), and had contracted their sentiments. — "The foregoing verses were really extempore, but a little corrected since."— *B.*

EPISTLE TO MAJOR LOGAN.

In the course of his visits to Ayr, Burns had formed an acquaintance with Major William Logan, a retired military officer, noted for his wit, his violin-playing, and his convivial habits, who lived a cheerful bachelor-life with his mother and an unmarried sister. Burns had visited Logan at his villa of Park, near Ayr, had enjoyed his fiddle and his waggery, and run over — so to speak — the whole gamut of his congenial heart. He had also been much pleased with the manners of the old lady and her daughter. On the 30th of October, he is found addressing the major in an epistle expressed in merry but careless verse.

HAIL, thairm-inspirin', rattlin' Willie! cat-gut
Though Fortune's road be rough and hilly
To every fiddling, rhyming billie, fellow
We never heed,
But take it like the unbacked filly,
Proud o' her speed.

When idly goavan whyles we saunter, walking aimlessly
Yirr, fancy barks, awa' we canter
Uphill, down brae, till some mischanter, accident
Some black bog-hole,
Arrests us, then the scaith and banter damage
We're forced to thole. bear

Hale be your heart! — hale be your fiddle!
Lang may your elbock jink and diddle,
To cheer you through the weary widdle struggle
O' this wild warl',
Until you on a crummock driddle staff — creep
A gray-haired carle.

Come wealth, come poortith, late or soon, poverty
Heaven send your heart-strings aye in tune,
And screw your temper-pins aboon, above
A fifth or mair,
The melancholious, lazy croon,
O' cankrie care.

May still your life from day to day
Nae "lente largo" in the play,
But "allegretto forte" gay
Harmonious flow,
A sweeping, kindling, bauld Strathspey —
Encore! Bravo!

A blessing on the cheery gang
Wha dearly like a jig or sang,
And never think o' right and wrang
By square and rule,
But as the clegs o' feeling stang, gadflies
Are wise or fool.

My hand-waled curse keep hard in chase chosen
The harpy, hoodock, purse-proud race, miserly

Wha count on poortith as disgrace!
Their tuneless hearts —
May fireside discords jar a base
To a' their parts!

But come, your hand, my careless brither,
I' th' ither' warl', if there's anither —
And that there is I've little swither — doubt
About the matter —
We cheek for chow shall jog thegither; — jole
I'se ne'er bid better. — expect

We've faults and failings — granted clearly,
We're frail backsliding mortals merely,
Eve's bonny squad priests wyte them — blame
sheerly — smartly
For our grand fa';
But still, but still — I like them dearly —
God bless them a'!

Ochon for poor Castalian drinkers,
When they fa' foul o' earthly jinkers, — sprightly girls
The witching cursed delicious blinkers
Hae put me hyte, — mad
And gart me weet my waukrife — made — sleepless
winkers
Wi' girnin' spite. — grinning

But by yon moon! — and that's high swearin' —
And every star within my hearin'!

And by her een wha was a dear ane!
I'll ne'er forget;
I hope to gie the jads a clearin' jades
In fair-play yet.

My loss I mourn, but not repent it,
I'll seek my pursie whare I tint it; lost
Ance to the Indies I were wonted, gone
Some cantrip hour, witching
By some sweet elf I'll yet be dinted, smitten
Then, *vive l'amour!*

Faites mes baise-mains respectueuses,
To sentimental sister Susie,
And honest Lucky; no to roose you, praise
Ye may be proud,
That sic a couple Fate allows ye
To grace your blood.

Nae mair at present can I measure,
And trowth, my rhymin' ware's nae treasure;
But when in Ayr, some half-hour's leisure,
Be't light, be't dark,
Sir Bard will do himself the pleasure
To call at Park.

R. B.

MOSSIGEL, 30*th October*, 1786.

AN EXPOSTULATION ON A REBUKE ADMINISTERED BY MRS. LAWRIE.

Rusticity's ungainly form
  May cloud the highest mind;
But when the heart is nobly warm,
  The good excuse will find.

Propriety's cold cautious rules
  Warm Fervour may o'erlook;
But spare poor Sensibility
  The ungentle, harsh rebuke.

ADDRESS TO EDINBURGH.

Edina! Scotia's darling seat!
  All hail thy palaces and towers,
Where once beneath a monarch's feet
  Sat Legislation's sovereign powers!
From marking wildly-scattered flowers,
  As on the banks of Ayr I strayed,
And singing, lone, the lingering hours,
  I shelter in thy honoured shade.

Here wealth still swells the golden tide,
  As busy Trade his labour plies;
There Architecture's noble pride
  Bids elegance and splendour rise;
Here Justice, from her native skies,
  High wields her balance and her rod;
There Learning, with his eagle eyes,
  Seeks Science in her coy abode.

Thy sons, Edina! social, kind,
  With open arms the stranger hail;
Their views enlarged, their liberal mind,
  Above the narrow, rural vale;
Attentive still to Sorrow's wail,
  Or modest Merit's silent claim;
And never may their sources fail!
  And never envy blot their name!

Thy daughters bright thy walks adorn,
  Gay as the gilded summer sky,
Sweet as the dewy milk-white thorn,
  Dear as the raptured thrill of joy!
Fair Burnet[1] strikes th' adoring eye,
  Heaven's beauties on my fancy shine;

[1] "Fair B. is heavenly Miss Burnet, daughter to Lord Monboddo, at whose house I have had the honour to be more than once. There has not been anything nearly like her in all the combinations of beauty, grace, and goodness the great Creator has formed since Milton's Eve on the first day of her existence."—*B.*

I see the Sire of Love on high,
  And own his work indeed divine!

There, watching high the least alarms,
  Thy rough, rude fortress gleams afar;
Like some bold veteran, gray in arms,
  And marked with many a seamy scar.
The ponderous wall and massy bar,
  Grim-rising o'er the rugged rock,
Have oft withstood assailing war,
  And oft repelled the invader's shock.

With awe-struck thought, and pitying tears,
  I view that noble, stately dome,
Where Scotia's kings of other years,
  Famed heroes! had their royal home.
Alas, how changed the times to come!
  Their royal name low in the dust!
Their hapless race wild wandering roam,
  Though rigid law cries out, 'Twas just!

Wild beats my heart to trace your steps,
  Whose ancestors, in days of yore,
Through hostile ranks and ruined gaps
  Old Scotia's bloody lion bore.
Even I who sing in rustic lore,
  Haply, my sires have left their shed,
And faced grim danger's loudest roar,
  Bold-following where your fathers led!

Edina! Scotia's darling seat!
All hail thy palaces and towers,
Where once beneath a monarch's feet
Sat Legislation's sovereign powers!
From marking wildly-scattered flowers,
As on the banks of Ayr I strayed,
And singing, lone, the lingering hours,
I shelter in thy honoured shade.

ODE ON THE CHEVALIER'S BIRTHDAY.

We have Burns's own authority for saying, that Jacobitism was not a deep feeling in his mind. It was, nevertheless, a sentiment which he at this time took no pains to conceal. A romantic feeling regarding his country, and its ancient independent condition, an antipathy towards the representatives of the old religious Whigs of Scotland, a sympathy springing from his own circumstances with all that was depressed by or in opposition to fortune — perhaps a shade of manly impatience with the cant of loyalty, as indulged in at that day — appear to have combined, with some notion about his own ancestral history, to throw Burns into this vain and insubstantial profession. Charles Edward was still alive, but lost in the sottishness which so sadly fell upon a mind once ardent and apparently capable of better things. A few generous souls, perhaps none of them of very high standing in society, kept his memory alive by an annual symposium on his birthday [Dec. 31]. Burns attending one of these occasions, acted in the capacity of poet-laureate, and produced an ode, of which Dr. Currie has preserved a few stanzas.

* * * *

FALSE flatterer, Hope, away![1]
Nor think to lure us as in days of yore;
We solemnise this sorrowing natal-day
To prove our loyal truth; we can no more;
And owning Heaven's mysterious sway,
Submissive low adore.

Ye honoured mighty dead!
Who nobly perished in the glorious cause,
Your king, your country, and her laws!
From great Dundee who smiling victory led,
And fell a martyr in her arms
(What breast of northern ice but warms?)
To bold Balmerino's undying name,
Whose soul of fire, lighted at heaven's high flame,
Deserves the proudest wreath departed heroes claim.

Nor unavenged your fate shall be,
It only lags the fatal hour;
Your blood shall with incessant cry

[1] "In the first part of this ode there is some beautiful imagery, which the poet afterwards interwove in the *Chevalier's Lament.*"—CURRIE.

Awake at last th' unsparing power;
As from the cliff, with thundering course,
The snowy ruin smokes along,
With doubling speed, and gathering force,
Till deep it crashing whelms the cottage in the
vale!

So vengeance * * * * *

TO MISS LOGAN[1] WITH BEATTIE'S POEMS:

AS A NEW-YEAR'S GIFT, JANUARY 1, 1787.

AGAIN the silent wheels of time
Their annual round have driven,
And you, though scarce in maiden prime,
Are so much nearer heaven.

No gifts have I from Indian coasts
The infant year to hail;
I send you more than India boasts
In Edwin's simple tale.

[1] Sister of Major Logan, to whom the poet had addressed an epistle on the 30th October of the past year.

Our sex with guile and faithless love
  Is charged, perhaps, too true;
But may, dear maid, each lover prove
  An Edwin still to you!

BONNIE DOON.*

This song referred to an unhappy love-story of which young Peggy K. was the heroine. See vol. i. p. 203. Another copy, considerably altered, is afterwards introduced.

January, 1787.

YE flowery banks o' bonnie Doon,
  How can ye bloom sae fair!
How can ye chant, ye little birds,
  And I sae fu' o' care!

Thou'll break my heart, thou bonnie bird,
  That sings upon the bough;
Thou minds me o' the happy days
  When my fause luve was true.

Thou'll break my heart, thou bonnie bird,
  That sings beside thy mate;
For sae I sat, and sae I sang,
  And wistna o' my fate. knew not

Aft hae I roved by bonnie Doon,
  To see the woodbine twine,
And ilka bird sang o' its love,
  And sae did I o' mine.

Wi' lightsome heart I pu'd a rose
  Frae aff its thorny tree,
And my fause luver staw the rose,
  But left the thorn wi' me.

THE GUDEWIFE OF WAUCHOPE-HOUSE TO BURNS.

During the first blaze of Burns's reputation in Edinburgh, several rhyming epistles were addressed to him publicly and privately — generally of no other value than to show how immensely he had stepped beyond all common bounds of success in cultivating the rustic Muse. One, however, from a Mrs. Scott of Wauchope, in Roxburghshire, was neatly and effectively written, and to it Burns made a suitable reply.

My cantie, witty, rhyming ploughman,
I hafflins doubt it is na true, man, half
That ye between the stilts was bred, plough-handles
Wi' ploughmen schooled, wi' ploughmen fed;
I doubt it sair, ye've drawn your knowledge
Either frae grammar-school or college.

Guid troth, your saul and body baith
War better fed, I'd gie my aith,
Than theirs who sup sour milk and parritch,
And bummil through the single bungle
Carritch. Catechism
Whaever heard the ploughman speak,
Could tell gif Homer was a Greek?
He'd flee as soon upon a cudgel,
As get a single line of Virgil.
And then sae slee ye crack your jokes
O' Willie Pitt and Charlie Fox,
Our great men a' sae weel descrive,
And how to gar the nation thrive, make
Ane maist wad swear ye dwalt amang them,
And as ye saw them, sae ye sang them.
But be ye ploughman, be ye peer,
Ye are a funny blade, I swear;
And though the cauld I ill can bide, endure
Yet twenty miles and mair I'd ride
O'er moss and moor, and never grumble,
Though my auld yad should gie a stumble, jade
To crack a winter night wi' thee,
And hear thy sangs and sonnets slee. sly
Oh gif I kenn'd but whare ye baide, resided
I'd send to you a marled plaid; checkered
'Twad haud your shouthers warm and braw,
And douce at kirk or market shaw; respectable
Fra' south as weel as north, my lad,
A' honest Scotsmen lo'e the maud. shepherd's plaid

BURNS TO THE GUDEWIFE OF WAUCHOPE-HOUSE.

I MIND it weel in early date,
When I was beardless, young, and blate, bashful
And first could thrash the barn,
Or haud a yokin' at the pleugh, bout
And though forfoughten sair eneugh, fatigued
Yet unco proud to learn:
When first among the yellow corn
A man I reckoned was,
And wi' the lave ilk merry morn rest
Could rank my rig and lass,
Still shearing, and clearing,
The tither stookèd raw, row
Wi claivers, and haivers, merry nonsense
Wearing the day awa'.

E'en then, a wish, I mind its power—
A wish that to my latest hour
Shall strongly heave my breast—
That I, for poor auld Scotland's sake,
Some usefu' plan or beuk could make,
Or sing a sang at least.
The rough burr-thissle, spreading wide
Amang the bearded bear, barley
I turned the weeder-clips aside,

And spared the symbol dear!
No nation, no station,
My envy e'er could raise,
A Scot still, but blot still,
I knew nae higher praise.

But still the elements o' sang,
In formless jumble, right and wrang,
Wild floated in my brain;
Till on that har'st I said before, harvest
My partner in the merry core,
She roused the forming strain.
I see her yet, the sonsie quean, comely
That lighted up my jingle,
Her witching smile, her pauky een sly
That gart my heart-strings tingle:
I firèd, inspirèd,
At every kindling keek, peep
But bashing, and dashing,
I fearèd aye to speak.

Health to the sex, ilk guid chiel says,
Wi' merry dance in winter days,
And we to share in common:
The gust o' joy, the balm of wo,
The saul o' life, the heaven below,
Is rapture-giving woman.
Ye surly sumphs, who hate the name, fools
Be mindfu' o' your mither;
She, honest woman, may think shame

That ye're connected with her.
Ye're wae men, ye're nae men woful
That slight the lovely dears;
To shame ye, disclaim ye,
Ilk honest birkie swears. fellow

For you, no bred to barn and byre, cow-house
Wha sweetly tune the Scottish lyre,
Thanks to you for your line:
The marled plaid ye kindly spare, checkered
By me should gratefully be ware; worn
'Twad please me to the Nine.
I'd be mair vauntie o' my hap, covering
Douce hingin' owre my curple, rump
Than ony ermine ever lap, wrapped
Or proud imperial purple.
Fareweel then, lang heal then, health
And plenty be your fa', lot
May losses and crosses
Ne'er at your hallan ca'! door

WILLIAM SMELLIE.

Burns was introduced by his printer to one of those convivial clubs composed of men of good condition which then abounded in Edinburgh, each usually founded upon some whim or conceit which shone through all its proceedings. The club in question assumed the name of the Crochallan Fencibles, from a composite cause. Its landlord Douglas was noted for singing a beautiful Gaelic song called *Crochallan* (properly, *Cro Chalein* — that is, Colin's Cattle). This, with the raising of fencible regiments going on at the time to protect the country while the army was chiefly engaged in fighting the American colonists, had given the convivial society an appellation. It was customary to subject a new entrant to a severe ordeal of raillery, by way of proving his temper, and Burns acknowledged that on that happening to himself, he had been "thrashed" in a style beyond all his experience. Here Burns met several of the men whose acquaintance he had previously made at the Canongate Kilwinning Lodge, particularly one William Dunbar, an uncommonly merry uproarious good fellow, who in the hours of mirthful relaxation appeared as *Colonel of the Crochallans*, but in the moments of daylight sobriety, practised as a douce writer to the Signet, from which position he ultimately stepped up to the dignity of Inspector-general of Stamp-duties for Scotland. William Smellie, the printer, has been thus described by Burns.

——————— To Crochallan came,
The old cocked-hat, the gray surtout, the same;
His bristling beard just rising in its might;
'Twas four long nights and days till shaving-night;
His uncombed grizzly locks, wild staring, thatched

A head for thought profound and clear unmatched;
Yet though his caustic wit was biting rude,
His heart was warm, benevolent, and good.

RATTLIN', ROARIN' WILLIE.

Willie Dunbar was commemorated in verses of a different strain. There was an old rough Border ditty referring to a certain *Rattling, Roaring Willie*, of great celebrity in his day as a wandering violer. To this Burns added a stanza, which we are to take as a picture of the Colonel in his place of command and moment of highest exaltation.

As I cam by Crochallan,
  I cannilie keekit ben; slyly peeped in
Rattlin', roarin' Willie
  Was sitting at yon boord-en';
Sitting at yon boord-en',
  And amang gude companie;
Rattlin', roarin' Willie,
  Ye're welcome hame to me!

INSCRIPTION FOR THE GRAVE OF FERGUSSON.

HERE LIES ROBERT FERGUSSON, POET.

BORN, SEPTEMBER 5TH, 1751 — DIED, 16TH OCTOBER, 1774.

No sculptured marble here, nor pompous lay,
  "No storied urn, nor animated bust;"
This simple stone directs pale Scotia's way
  To pour her sorrows o'er her Poet's dust.

VERSES UNDER THE PORTRAIT OF FERGUSSON.

The keen sympathy felt by Burns for Fergusson was expressed on many occasions. Very soon after making the arrangements for the tombstone (March 19, 1787), he presented a copy of the works of the Edinburgh poet to a young lady, and wrote the following lines under the portrait which served for a frontispiece.

Curse on ungrateful man, that can be pleased,
And yet can starve the author of the pleasure!
Oh thou, my elder brother in misfortune,

By far my elder brother in the Muses,
With tears I pity thy unhappy fate!
Why is the bard unpitied by the world,
Yet has so keen a relish of its pleasures?

VERSES INTENDED TO BE WRITTEN BELOW A NOBLE EARL'S PICTURE. [THE EARL OF GLENCAIRN.]

WHOSE is that noble, dauntless brow?
And whose that eye of fire?
And whose that generous princely mien
Even rooted foes admire?

Stranger, to justly shew that brow,
And mark that eye of fire,
Would takė His hand, whose vernal tints
His other works admire.

Bright as a cloudless summer sun,
With stately port he moves;
His guardian seraph eyes with awe
The noble ward he loves.

Among the illustrious Scottish sons
That chief thou may'st discern;
Mark Scotia's fond returning eye,
It dwells upon Glencairn.

THE AMERICAN WAR.

A FRAGMENT.

WHEN Guildford good our pilot stood,
  And did our helm thraw, man, — turn
Ae night, at tea, began a plea, — quarrel
  Within America, man:
Then up they gat the maskin'-pat, — tea-pot
  And in the sea did jaw, man; — dash
And did nae less, in full Congréss,
  Than quite refuse our law, man.

Then through the lakes Montgomery[1] takes,
  I wat he was na slaw, man;
Down Lowrie's Burn[2] he took a turn,
  And Carleton did ca', man; — drive before him
But yet, what-reck, he, at Quebec, — what matters
  Montgomery-like[3] did fa', man,
Wi' sword in hand, before his band,
  Amang his en'mies a', man.

1 General Richard Montgomery invaded Canada, autumn 1775, and took Montreal, the British commander, Sir Guy Carleton, retiring before him. In an attack on Quebec he was less fortunate, being killed by a storm of grape-shot in leading on his men at Cape Diamond.

2 Lowrie's Burn, a pseudonyme for the St. Lawrence.

3 A passing compliment to the Montgomeries of Coilsfield, the patrons of the poet.

Poor Tammy Gage, within a cage,
  Was kept at Boston ha', man ; [1]
Till Willie Howe took o'er the knowe — knoll
  For Philadelphia,[2] man.
Wi' sword and gun he thought a sin
  Guid Christian blood to draw, man :
But at New York, wi' knife and fork,
  Sir-loin he hackèd sma',[3] man.

Burgoyne gaed up, like spur and whip,
  Till Fraser brave did fa', man ;
Then lost his way, ae misty day,
  In Saratoga shaw, man. — wood
Cornwallis fought as lang's he dought, — could
  And did the buckskins claw, man ;
But Clinton's glaive frae rust to save, — sword
  He hung it to the wa', man.

Then Montague, and Guildford too,
  Began to fear a fa', man ;
And Sackville dour, wha stood the — obdurate
    stoure, — dust

[1] General Gage, governor of Massachusetts, was cooped up in Boston by General Washington during the latter part of 1775 and early part of 1776. In consequence of his inefficiency, he was replaced in October of that year by General Howe.

[2] General Howe removed his army from New York to Philadelphia in the summer of 1777.

[3] Alluding to a *razzia* made by orders of Howe at Peekskill, March 1777, when a large quantity of cattle belonging to the Americans was destroyed.

The German Chief to thraw, man: thwart
For Paddy Burke, like ony Turk,
Nae mercy had at a', man;
And Charlie Fox threw by the box,
And lowsed his tinkler jaw, man. loosed

Then Rockingham took up the game,
Till death did on him ca', man;
When Shelburne meek held up his cheek,
Conform to gospel law, man.
Saint Stephen's boys, wi' jarring noise,
They did his measures thraw, man,
For North and Fox united stocks,
And bore him to the wa', man.[1]

Then clubs and hearts were Charlie's cartes,
He swept the stakes awa', man,
Till the diamond's ace, of Indian race,
Led him a sair *faux pas*,[2] man.
The Saxon lads, wi' loud placads, cheers
On Chatham's boy did ca', man;

[1] Lord North's administration was succeeded by that of the Marquis of Rockingham, March, 1782. At the death of the latter in the succeeding July, Lord Shelburne became prime minister, and Mr. Fox resigned his secretaryship. Under his lordship, peace was restored, January, 1783. By the union of Lord North and Mr. Fox, Lord Shelburne was soon after forced to resign in favor of his rivals, the heads of the celebrated Coalition.

[2] Fox's famous India Bill, by which his ministry was brought to destruction, December, 1783.

And Scotland drew her pipe, and blew,
  "Up, Willie, waur them a', man!" vanquish

Behind the throne then Grenville's gone,
  A secret word or twa, man;
While slee Dundas aroused the class,
  Be-north the Roman Wa', man:
And Chatham's wraith, in heavenly graith, armor
  (Inspired bardies saw, man,)
Wi' kindling eyes cried: "Willie, rise!
  Would I hae feared them a', man?"

But, word and blow, North, Fox, and Co.,
  Gowff'd Willie like a ba', man, struck
Till Suthron raise, and coost their claise cast off
  Behind him in a raw, man;
And Caledon threw by the drone,
  And did her whittle draw, man; knife
And swoor fu' rude, through dirt and blood,
  To make it guid in law, man.[1]

* * * * *

[1] In the new parliament called by Mr. Pitt, after his accession to office, in the spring of 1784, amidst the many new members brought in for his support, and that of the king's prerogative, there was an exceeding proportion from Scotland.

TO A HAGGIS.[1]

Fair fa' your honest, sonsie face, plump
Great chieftain o' the puddin'-race:
Aboon them a' ye tak your place,
Painch, tripe, or thairm; small guts
Weel are ye wordy of a grace worthy
As lang's my arm.

The groaning trencher there ye fill,
Your hurdies like a distant hill; haunches
Your pin wad help to mend a mill
In time o' need,
While through your pores the dews distil
Like amber bead.

His knife see rustic labour dight, make ready
And cut you up wi' ready slight,
Trenching your gushing entrails bright
Like ony ditch;
And then, oh what a glorious sight,
Warm-reekin', rich!

[1] The haggis is a dish peculiar to Scotland, though supposed to be of French extraction. It is composed of minced offal of mutton, mixed with oatmeal and suet, and boiled in a sheep's stomach. When made in *Elspa's* way, with "a curn o' spice" (see the *Gentle Shepherd*), it is an agreeable, albeit a somewhat heavy dish, always providing that no horror be felt at the idea of its preparation.

Then horn for horn they stretch and strive,
Deil tak the hindmost, on they drive,
Till a' their weel-swall'd kytes swelled stomachs
belyve by and by
Are bent like drums;
Then auld guidman, maist like to rive, burst
"Bethankit!" hums.

Is there that owre his French ragout,
Or olio that wad staw a sow, surfeit
Or fricassee wad mak her spew
Wi' perfect scunner, disgust
Looks down wi' sneering, scornfu' view
On sic a dinner!

Poor devil! see him owre his trash,
As feckless as a withered rash, feeble
His spindle-shank a guid whip-lash,
His nieve a nit; fist — nut
Through bloody flood or field to dash,
Oh how unfit!

But mark the rustic, haggis-fed,
The trembling earth resounds his tread,
Clap in his walie nieve a blade, lusty fist
He'll mak it whissle;
And legs, and arms, and heads will sned, shear
Like taps o' thrissle. thistle

Ye Powers wha mak mankind your care,
And dish them out their bill o' fare,

Auld Scotland wants nae skinking ware — thin stuff
That jaups in luggies; — splashes in bowls
But, if ye wish her gratefu' prayer,
Gie her a Haggis!

EXTEMPORE IN THE COURT OF SESSION.

TUNE — *Killiecrankie.*

Two well-drawn sketches of the leading barristers of that day — namely, the Dean of Faculty, Harry Erskine, and the Lord Advocate, Mr. Ilay Campbell (subsequently Lord President).

LORD ADVOCATE.

HE clenched his pamphlets in his fist,
He quoted and he hinted,
Till in a declamation-mist,
His argument he tint it: — lost
He gapèd for't, he graipèd for't, — groped
He fand it was awa', man;
But what his common-sense came short,
He ekèd out wi' law, man.

MR. ERSKINE.

Collected Harry stood a wee,
Then opened out his arm, man;
His lordship sat wi' ruefu' e'e,
And eyed the gathering storm, man;

Like wind-driven hail, it did assail,
  Or torrents owre a linn, man; waterfall
The Bench sae wise lift up their eyes,
  Half-wauken'd wi' the din, man.

PROLOGUE SPOKEN BY MR. WOODS ON HIS BENEFIT-NIGHT,

Monday, 16th April, 1787.

Amongst the men whom Burns had met and liked at the Canongate Kilwinning Lodge, was Joseph Woods, a respectable member of the Edinburgh *corps dramatique*, and the more likely to be endeared to the Ayrshire poet, that he had been an intimate friend of poor Fergusson.

When by a generous Public's kind acclaim,
That dearest meed is granted — honest Fame;
When here your favour is the actor's lot,
Nor even the man in private life forgot;
What breast so dead to heavenly Virtue's glow,
But heaves impassioned with the grateful throe?

  Poor is the task to please a barbarous throng,
It needs no Siddons' powers in Southern's song;
But here an ancient nation famed afar,

For genius, learning high, as great in war —
Hail, CALEDONIA, name for ever dear!
Before whose sons I'm honoured to appear!
Where every science — every nobler art —
That can inform the mind, or mend the heart,
Is known; as grateful nations oft have found
Far as the rude barbarian marks the bound.
Philosophy, no idle pedant dream,
Here holds her search by heaven-taught Reason's beam;
Here History paints with elegance and force
The tide of Empire's fluctuating course;
Here Douglas forms wild Shakspeare into plan,
And Harley[1] rouses all the god in man.
When well-formed taste and sparkling wit unite
With manly lore, or female beauty bright
(Beauty, where faultless symmetry and grace,
Can only charm us in the second place)
Witness my heart, how oft with panting fear,
As on this night, I've met these judges here!
But still the hope Experience taught to live,
Equal to judge — you're candid to forgive.
No hundred-headed Riot here we meet,
With Decency and Law beneath his feet;
Nor Insolence assumes fair Freedom's name;
Like CALEDONIANS, you applaud or blame.

Oh thou dread Power! whose empire-giving hand

[1] *The Man of Feeling*, written by Mr. Mackenzie.

Has oft been stretched to shield the honoured
land!
Strong may she glow with all her ancient fire!
May every son be worthy of his sire!
Firm may she rise with generous disdain
At Tyranny's or direr Pleasure's chain!
Still self-dependent in her native shore,
Bold may she brave grim Danger's loudest
roar,
Till Fate the curtain drops on worlds to be no
more!

WILLIE'S AWA'.

"The enclosed I have just wrote, nearly extempore, in a solitary inn at Selkirk, after a miserably wet day's riding." — *Burns to William Creech*, 13*th May*, 1787.

AULD chuckie[1] Reekie's[2] sair distrest,
Down droops her ance weel-burnished crest,
Nae joy her bonny buskit nest (decorated)
Can yield ava, (at all)
Her darling bird that she lo'es best —
Willie's awa'!

[1] Literally, a hen; secondarily, a familiar term of address:

"Gin ony sour-mou'd girning bucky
Ca' me conceited keckling chucky." — RAMSAY.

[2] Literally, smoky; a familiar sobriquet for Edinburgh, not at all unsuitable.

Oh Willie was a witty wight,
And had o' things an unco slight; knowledge
Auld Reekie aye he keepit tight,
And trig and braw:
But now they'll busk her like a fright — dress
Willie's awa'!

The stiffest o' them a' he bowed;
The bauldest o' them a' he cowed;
They durst nae mair than he allowed,
That was a law:
We've lost a birkie weel worth gowd — fellow — gold
Willie's awa'!

Now gawkies, tawpies, gowks,[1] and fools,
Frae colleges and boarding-schools,
May sprout like simmer puddock-stools toad-stools
In glen or shaw; wood
He wha could brush them down to
mools — the dust
Willie's awa'!

The brethren o' the Commerce-Chaumer[2]
May mourn their loss wi' doolfu' clamour;
He was a dictionar and grammar
Amang them a';

[1] Gawky, a simpleton; tawpy, usually applied to a foolish, sluttish woman; gowk, literally, the cuckoo; secondarily, a fool.

[2] The Chamber of Commerce at Edinburgh, of which Creech was secretary.

I fear they'll now mak monie a stammer —
    Willie's awa'!

Nae mair we see his levee door [1]
Philosophers and poets pour,
And toothy critics by the score,
    In bloody raw! row
The adjutant o' a' the core —
    Willie's awa'!

Now worthy Gregory's Latin face,
Tytler's and Greenfield's modest grace,
Mackenzie, Stewart, sic a brace
    As Rome ne'er saw;
They a' maun meet some ither place —
    Willie's awa'!

Poor Burns e'en Scotch drink canna quicken;
He cheeps like some bewildered chicken, chirps

[1] Creech, who, besides being a clever and well-educated man, enjoyed high reputation as a teller of quaint stories, lived on familiar terms with many of the literary men of his day. His house, in one of the elevated floors of a tenement in the High Street, accessible from a wretched alley called Craig's Close, was frequented in the mornings by company of that kind, to such an extent that the meeting used to be called *Creech's Levee.* Burns here enumerates as attending it, Dr. James Gregory, author of the *Conspectus Medicinæ;* Alexander Fraser Tytler, afterwards Lord Woodhouselee; Dr. William Greenfield, professor of rhetoric in the Edinburgh University; Henry Mackenzie, author of *The Man of Feeling;* and Dugald Stewart, professor of moral philosophy.

Scared frae its minnie and the cleckin' — mother / brood
By hoodie-craw; — hooded-crow
Grief's gien his heart an unco kickin'—
Willie's awa'!

Now every sour-mou'd girnin' blellum— — grinning / talking fellow
And Calvin's folk, are fit to fell him;
And self-conceited critic skellum [1]
His quill may draw;
He wha could brawlie ward their bellum—
Willie's awa'!

Up wimpling stately Tweed I've sped, — winding
And Eden scenes on crystal Jed,
And Ettrick banks now roaring red,
While tempests blaw;
But every joy and pleasure's fled—
Willie's awa'!

May I be Slander's common speech,
A text for infamy to preach,
And lastly, streekit out to bleach — stretched
In winter snaw,
When I forget thee, Willie Creech,
Though far awa'!

[1] A term of contempt:

"She tauld thee weel, thou was a skellum."

Tam o' Shanter.

May never wicked Fortune touzle him! teaze
May never wicked men bamboozle him!
Until a pow as auld's Methusalem
He canty claw! cheerfully scratch
Then to the blessèd New Jerusalem
Fleet wing awa'!

ON INCIVILITY SHEWN HIM AT INVERARY.

The Duke of Argyle had an overabundance of guests in the castle, and the innkeeper at Inverary was too much occupied with the surplus to have any attention to spare for passing travellers. Hereupon Burns penned an epigram, which it is to be supposed he left inscribed on one of the windows. We must regret this as a discourtesy towards a most respectable nobleman — the more so, as the names of the Duke and Duchess of Argyle stand at the head of the subscription for his Poems.

WHOE'ER he be that sojourns here,
I pity much his case,
Unless he come to wait upon
The Lord their God — his Grace.

There's naething here but Highland pride,
And Highland scab and hunger;
If Providence has sent me here,
'Twas surely in an anger.

COMPOSED ON LEAVING A PLACE IN THE HIGHLANDS WHERE HE HAD BEEN KINDLY ENTERTAINED.

When Death's dark stream I ferry o'er —
A time that surely shall come —
In Heaven itself I'll ask no more,
Than just a Highland welcome!

ON READING IN A NEWSPAPER

THE DEATH OF JOHN M'LEOD, Esq.,

BROTHER TO A YOUNG LADY, A PARTICULAR FRIEND OF THE AUTHOR'S.

Sad thy tale, thou idle page,
And rueful thy alarms:
Death tears the brother of her love
From Isabella's arms.

Sweetly decked with pearly dew
  The morning rose may blow,
But cold successive noontide blasts
  May lay its beauties low.

Fair on Isabella's morn
  The sun propitious smiled,
But, long ere noon, succeeding clouds
  Succeeding hopes beguiled.

Fate oft tears the bosom cords
  That nature finest strung;
So Isabella's heart was formed,
  And so that heart was wrung.

Were it in the poet's power,
  Strong as he shares the grief
That pierces Isabella's heart,
  To give that heart relief!

Dread Omnipotence alone
  Can heal the wound he gave,
Can point the brimful grief-worn eyes
  To scenes beyond the grave.

Virtue's blossoms there shall blow,
  And fear no withering blast;
There Isabella's spotless worth
  Shall happy be at last.

ON THE DEATH OF SIR JAMES HUNTER BLAIR.

Sir James was an Ayrshire squire, and a member of the banking-house of Sir William Forbes and Company; a public-spirited citizen and magistrate of Edinburgh, and an amiable man. He had been one of Burns's kindest patrons when the poet first came to town, feeling, doubtless, a particular interest in his fortunes on account of his Ayrshire nativity.

THE lamp of day, with ill-presaging glare,
Dim, cloudy, sank beneath the western wave;
The inconstant blast howled through the darkening air,
And hollow whistled in the rocky cave.

Lone as I wandered by each cliff and dell,
Once the loved haunts of Scotia's royal train;[1]
Or mused where limpid streams once hallowed well,[2]
Or mouldering ruins mark the sacred fane;[3]

The increasing blast roared round the beetling rocks,
The clouds, swift-winged, flew o'er the starry sky,

[1] The King's Park, at Holyrood House.
[2] St. Anthony's Well. [3] St. Anthony's Chapel.

The groaning trees untimely shed their locks,
  And shooting-meteors caught the startled eye.

The paly moon rose in the livid east,
  And 'mong the cliffs disclosed a stately form,
In weeds of wo that frantic beat her breast,
  And mixed her wailings with the raving storm.

Wild to my heart the filial pulses glow,
  'Twas Caledonia's trophied shield I viewed:
Her form majestic drooped in pensive wo,
  The lightning of her eye in tears imbued.

Reversed that spear, redoubtable in war,
  Reclined that banner, erst in fields unfurled,
That like a deathful meteor gleamed afar,
  And braved the mighty monarchs of the world.

"My patriot son fills an untimely grave!"
  With accents wild and lifted arms she cried:
"Low lies the hand that oft was stretched to save,
  Low lies the heart that swelled with honest pride.

"A weeping country joins a widow's tear;
  The helpless poor mix with the orphan's cry;
The drooping arts surround their patron's bier;
  And grateful science heaves the heartfelt sigh!

"I saw my sons resume their ancient fire;
  I saw fair Freedom's blossoms richly blow;
But ah! how hope is born but to expire!
  Relentless fate has laid their guardian low.

"My patriot falls: but shall he lie unsung,
  While empty greatness saves a worthless name?
No: every Muse shall join her tuneful tongue,
  And future ages hear his growing fame.

"And I will join a mother's tender cares,
  Through future times to make his virtue last;
That distant years may boast of other Blairs!"—
  She said, and vanished with the sweeping blast.

TO MISS FERRIER,[1]

ENCLOSING THE ELEGY ON SIR J. H. BLAIR.

NAE heathen name shall I prefix
  Frae Pindus or Parnassus;
Auld Reekie dings them a' to sticks, beats
  For rhyme-inspiring lasses.

Jove's tunefu' dochters three times three
  Made Homer deep their debtor;

[1] Author of *The Inheritance*, etc.

But, gien the body half an e'e, given
Nine Ferriers wad done better!

Last day my mind was in a bog,
Down George's Street I stoited; tottered
A creeping cauld prosaic fog
My very senses doited. stupefied

Do what I dought to set her free, could
My saul lay in the mire;
Ye turned a neuk — I saw your e'e —
She took the wing like fire!

The mournfu' sang I here enclose
In gratitude I send you;
And [wish and] pray in rhyme sincere,
A' gude things may attend you![1]

VERSES

WRITTEN WITH A PENCIL OVER THE CHIMNEY-PIECE, IN THE PARLOUR OF THE INN AT KENMORE, TAYMOUTH.

ADMIRING Nature in her wildest grace,
These northern scenes with weary feet I trace;
O'er many a winding dale and painful steep,
The abodes of covied grouse and timid sheep,

[1] The original manuscript of this piece is in the possession of Miss Grace Aiken, Ayr.

My savage journey, curious, I pursue,
Till famed Breadálbane opens to my view.
The meeting cliffs each deep-sunk glen divides,
The woods, wild scattered, clothe their ample sides;
The outstretching lake, imbosomed 'mong the hills,
The eye with wonder and amazement fills;
The Tay, meandering sweet in infant pride,
The palace, rising on its verdant side;
The lawns, wood-fringed in Nature's native taste;
The hillocks, dropt in Nature's careless haste;
The arches, striding o'er the new-born stream;
The village, glittering in the noontide beam—

* * * *

Poetic ardours in my bosom swell,
Lone wandering by the hermit's mossy cell:
The sweeping theatre of hanging woods;
The incessant roar of headlong tumbling floods—

* * * *

Here Poesy might wake her Heaven-taught lyre,
And look through nature with creative fire;
Here to the wrongs of Fate half reconciled,
Misfortune's lightened steps might wander wild;
And Disappointment, in these lonely bounds,
Find balm to soothe her bitter, rankling wounds:
Here heart-struck Grief might heavenward stretch her scan,
And injured Worth forget and pardon man.

* * * *

THE BIRKS OF ABERFELDY.

TUNE—*The Birks of Abergeldy.*

The beautiful falls of Moness, at Aberfeldy, excited the poet to verse; but on this occasion it came in a lyric form, for he remembered a simple old ditty, called the *Birks of Abergeldy*, referring to a place in Aberdeenshire, and struck by the nearly identical name of this spot, his thoughts fell into harmony with the tune possessing his mind.

CHORUS.

BONNY lassie, will ye go,
Will ye go, will ye go?
Bonny lassie, will ye go
To the birks of Aberfeldy?

Now simmer blinks on flowery braes, glances
And o'er the crystal streamlet plays;
Come, let us spend the lightsome days
In the birks of Aberfeldy.

The little birdies blithely sing,
While o'er their heads the hazels hing, hang
Or lightly flit on wanton wing
In the birks of Aberfeldy.

The braes ascend, like lofty wa's,
The foamy stream deep-roaring fa's,
O'erhung wi' fragrant spreading shaws, woods
 The birks of Aberfeldy.

The hoary cliffs are crowned wi' flowers,
White o'er the linns the burnie pours, cascades
And rising, weets wi' misty showers
 The birks of Aberfeldy.

Let Fortune's gifts at random flee,
They ne'er shall draw a wish frae me,
Supremely blest wi' love and thee,
 In the birks of Aberfeldy.

THE HUMBLE PETITION OF BRUAR WATER[1] TO THE NOBLE DUKE OF ATHOLE.

My lord, I know your noble ear
 Wo ne'er assails in vain;
Emboldened thus, I beg you'll hear
 Your humble slave complain,

[1] "The first object of interest that occurs upon the public road after leaving Blair, is a chasm in the hill on the right hand, through which the little river Bruar falls over a series of beautiful cascades. Formerly, the Falls of the Bruar were unadorned by wood; but the poet Burns, being conducted to

How saucy Phœbus' scorching beams,
  In flaming summer-pride,
Dry-withering, waste my foamy streams,
  And drink my crystal tide.

The lightly-jumpin' glowrin' trouts, staring
  That through my waters play,
If, in their random, wanton spouts,
  They near the margin stray;
If, hapless chance! they linger lang,
  I'm scorching up so shallow,
They're left the whitening stanes amang,
  In gasping death to wallow.

Last day I grat wi' spite and teen, wept—vexation
  As Poet Burns came by,
That to a bard I should be seen
  Wi' half my channel dry:
A panegyric rhyme, I ween,
  Even as I was he shored me; promised
But had I in my glory been,
  He, kneeling, wad adored me.

see them (September 1787,) after visiting the Duke of Athole, recommended that they should be invested with that necessary decoration. Accordingly, trees have been thickly planted along the chasm, and are now far advanced to maturity. Throughout this young forest a walk has been cut, and a number of fantastic little grottos erected for the conveniency of those who visit the spot. The river not only makes several distinct falls, but rushes on through a channel, whose roughness and haggard sublimity adds greatly to the merits of the scene, as an object of interest among tourists." — *Picture of Scotland.*

Here, foaming down the shelvy rocks,
  In twisting strength I rin;
There, high my boiling torrent smokes,
  Wild roaring o'er a linn: cascade
Enjoying large each spring and well,
  As Nature gave them me,
I am, although I say't mysel',
  Worth gaun a mile to see.

Would then my noble master please
  To grant my highest wishes,
He'll shade my banks wi' towering trees,
  And bonny spreading bushes.
Delighted doubly then, my lord,
  You'll wander on my banks,
And listen monie a grateful bird
  Return you tuneful thanks.

The sober laverock, warbling wild, lark
  Shall to the skies aspire;
The gowdspink, Music's gayest child, goldfinch
  Shall sweetly join the choir:
The blackbird strong, the lintwhite clear, linnet
  The mavis mild and mellow, thrush
The robin pensive autumn cheer,
  In all her locks of yellow.

This, too, a covert shall insure
  To shield them from the storm;
And coward maukin sleep secure, hare

Low in her grassy form.
Here shall the shepherd make his seat,
To weave his crown of flowers;
Or find a sheltering safe retreat
From prone descending showers.

And here, by sweet endearing stealth,
Shall meet the loving pair,
Despising worlds with all their wealth
As empty idle care.
The flowers shall vie in all their charms
The hour of heaven to grace,
And birks extend their fragrant arms
To screen the dear embrace.

Here haply too, at vernal dawn,
Some musing bard may stray,
And eye the smoking, dewy lawn,
And misty mountain gray;
Or by the reaper's nightly beam,
Mild-chequering through the trees,
Rave to my darkly dashing stream,
Hoarse swelling on the breeze.

Let lofty firs, and ashes cool,
My lowly banks o'erspread,
And view, deep bending in the pool,
Their shadows' watery bed!
Let fragrant birks in woodbines drest
My craggy cliffs adorn;

And, for the little songster's nest,
The close embowering thorn.

So may old Scotia's darling hope,
Your little angel band,
Spring, like their fathers, up to prop
Their honoured native land!
So may, through Albion's farthest ken,
To social-flowing glasses,
The grace be — "Athole's honest men,
And Athole's bonny lasses!"

VERSES

WRITTEN WHILE STANDING BY THE FALL OF FYERS, NEAR LOCH NESS.

Among the heathy hills and ragged woods,
The foaming Fyers pours his mossy floods;
Till full he dashes on the rocky mounds,
Where, through a shapeless breach, his stream resounds.
As high in air the bursting torrents flow,
As deep recoiling surges foam below;
Prone down the rock the whitening sheet descends,
And viewless Echo's ear, astonished, rends.

Dim seen, through rising mists and ceaseless
showers,
The hoary cavern, wide surrounding, lowers;
Still through the gap the struggling river toils,
And still below, the horrid caldron boils —

* * * *

CASTLE-GORDON.

Designed to be sung to *Morag*, a Highland tune, of which Burns was extremely fond. — CURRIE.

STREAMS that glide in Orient plains,
Never bound by Winter's chains;
Glowing here on golden sands,
There commixed with foulest stains,
From tyranny's empurpled bands;
These, their richly-gleaming waves,
I leave to tyrants and their slaves;
Give me the stream that sweetly laves
The banks by Castle-Gordon.

Spicy forests, ever gay,
Shading from the burning ray
Helpless wretches sold to toil,
Or the ruthless native's way,
Bent on, slaughter, blood, and spoil;
Woods that ever verdant wave,

I leave the tyrant and the slave;
Give me the groves that lofty brave
The storms by Castle-Gordon.

Wildly here, without control,
Nature reigns and rules the whole;
In that sober, pensive mood,
Dearest to the feeling soul,
She plants the forest, pours the flood.
Life's poor day I'll musing rave,
And find at night a sheltering cave,
Where waters flow and wild woods wave,
By bonny Castle-Gordon.

THE BONNY LASS OF ALBANY.

TUNE — *Mary's Dream.*

Journeying through the Highlands with a Jacobite companion, Burns could not but feel a little more enthusiastic than he generally did regarding the memory of the Stuarts. His visit to the natal district of those ancestors whom he believed to have followed the Cavalier standard, would give increased energy to his feelings of romantic loyalty. Connecting these considerations with the fact of Prince Charles having this very month, [Sept. 1787] declared the legitimacy of his hitherto supposed natural daughter, styled Duchess of Albany, I deem it probable that it was at this time that Burns composed a song in honor of that lady which has not till now seen the light.

MY heart is wae, and unco wae,
  To think upon the raging sea,
That roars between her gardens green
  And the bonny Lass of Albany.

This lovely maid's of royal blood
  That rulèd Albion's kingdoms three,
But oh, alas! for her bonny face,
  They've wranged the Lass of Albany.

In the rolling tide of spreading Clyde
  There sits an isle of high degree,[1]
And a town of fame whose princely name
  Should grace the Lass of Albany.[2]

But there's a youth, a witless youth,
  That fills the place where she should be;[3]
We'll send him o'er to his native shore,
  And bring our ain sweet Albany.

Alas the day, and wo the day,
  A false usurper wan the gree, superiority

[1] Bute.

[2] Rothsay, the county town of Bute, gave a title to the eldest sons of the kings of Scotland (Duke of Rothsay).

[3] An allusion to the Prince of Wales.

Who now commands the towers and lands,
  The royal right of Albany.

We'll daily pray, we'll nightly pray,
  On bended knees most fervently,
The time may come, with pipe and drum,
  We'll welcome hame fair Albany.[1]

ON SCARING SOME WATER-FOWL IN LOCH TURIT.

Why, ye tenants of the lake,
For me your watery haunt forsake?
Tell me, fellow-creatures, why
At my presence thus you fly?
Why disturb your social joys,
Parent, filial, kindred ties?—
Common friend to you and me,
Nature's gifts to all are free:
Peaceful keep your dimpling wave,
Busy feed, or wanton lave;
Or, beneath the sheltering rock,
Bide the surging billow's shock.

[1] Prince Charles, at his death in 1788, left the Duchess of Albany his sole heir, but she did not long survive him. The above song is printed from a portion of a manuscript book in Burns's handwriting, which is now in the possession of Mr. B. Nightingale, London.

Conscious, blushing for our race,
Soon, too soon, your fears I trace.
Man, your proud usurping foe,
Would be lord of all below:
Plumes himself in Freedom's pride,
Tyrant stern to all beside.
The eagle, from the cliffy brow,
Marking you his prey below,
In his breast no pity dwells,
Strong necessity compels:
But man, to whom alone is given
A ray direct from pitying Heaven,
Glories in his heart humane —
And creatures for his pleasure slain.
In these savage, liquid plains,
Only known to wandering swains,
Where the mossy riv'let strays,
Far from human haunts and ways,
All on Nature you depend,
And life's poor season peaceful spend.
Or, if man's superior might
Dare invade your native right,
On the lofty ether borne,
Man with all his powers you scorn;
Swiftly seek, on clanging wings,
Other lakes and other springs;
And the foe you cannot brave,
Scorn at least to be his slave.

BLITHE WAS SHE.

TUNE—*Andro and his Cutty Gun.*

The subject of these verses was Miss Euphemia Murray of Lintrose, a beautiful creature of eighteen, already distinguished by the *sobriquet* of the "Flower of Strathmore."

CHORUS.

BLITHE, blithe and merry was she,
  Blithe was she but and ben: *i. e.* everywhere
Blithe by the banks of Earn,
  And blithe in Glenturit Glen.

By Auchtertyre grows the aik, oak
  On Yarrow banks the birken shaw; birch-woods
But Phemie was a bonnier lass
  Than braes o' Yarrow ever saw.

Her looks were like a flower in May,
  Her smile was like a simmer morn;
She trippèd by the banks o' Earn,
  As light's a bird upon a thorn.

Her bonny face it was as meek
  As ony lamb upon a lea;

The evening sun was ne'er sae sweet
  As was the blink o' Phemie's e'e.

The Highland hills I've wandered wide,
  And o'er the lowlands I hae been ;
But Phemie was the blithest lass
  That ever trod the dewy green.

THE ROSE-BUD.

TUNE — *The Shepherd's Wife.*

Burns had taken up his residence with Mr. William Cruikshank, a master in the Edinburgh High School. Mr. Cruikshank had a daughter Janet, a young girl of budding loveliness, and much promise as a pianist. To her the poet was indebted for many pleasant hours, in listening to his favorite Scottish airs. He also employed her voice and instrument in enabling him to adapt new verses to old airs for the *Scots Musical Museum.* He gratefully celebrated his favorite, little Miss Jenny Cruikshank, in the two following pieces.

A ROSE-BUD by my early walk,
Adown a corn-enclosèd bawk,[1]
Sae gently bent its thorny stalk,
    All on a dewy morning.

[1] An open space in a cornfield, generally a ridge left untilled.

Ere twice the shades o' dawn are fled,
In a' its crimson glory spread,
And drooping rich the dewy head,
    It scents the early morning.

Within the bush, her covert nest,
A little linnet fondly prest,
The dew sat chilly on her breast
    Sae early in the morning.
She soon shall see her tender brood,
The pride, the pleasure o' the wood,
Amang the fresh green leaves bedewed,
    Awake the early morning.

So thou, dear bird, young Jenny fair!
On trembling string or vocal air,
Shall sweetly pay the tender care
    That tents thy early morning. guards
So thou, sweet Rose-bud, young and gay,
Shalt beauteous blaze upon the day,
And bless the parent's evening ray
    That watched thy early morning.

TO MISS CRUIKSHANK, A VERY YOUNG LADY,

WRITTEN ON THE BLANK-LEAF OF A BOOK PRESENTED TO HER BY THE AUTHOR.

BEAUTEOUS Rose-bud, young and gay,
Blooming in thy early May,
Never mayst thou, lovely flower,
Chilly shrink in sleety shower;
Never Boreas' hoary path,
Never Eurus' poisonous breath,
Never baleful stellar lights,
Taint thee with untimely blights!
Never, never reptile thief
Riot on thy virgin leaf,
Nor even Sol too fiercely view
Thy bosom blushing still with dew!

Mayst thou long, sweet crimson gem,
Richly deck thy native stem:
Till some evening, sober, calm,
Dropping dews and breathing balm,
While all around the woodland rings,
And every bird thy requiem sings,
Thou, amid the dirgeful sound,
Shed thy dying honours round,
And resign to parent earth
The loveliest form she e'er gave birth.

WHERE BRAVING ANGRY WINTER'S STORMS.

TUNE — *Neil Gow's Lamentation for Abercairny.*

The two following songs, in honor of Miss Margaret Chalmers, were designed for publication in the second volume of Johnson's *Museum.* Of the personal attractions of Miss Chalmers, it could at the utmost be said, as Burns did say, that they were above the medium. She was, however, a woman of spirit, talent, and boundless love of things literary.

WHERE, braving angry winter's storms,
  The lofty Ochils rise,
Far in their shade my Peggy's charms
  First blest my wondering eyes;
As one who by some savage stream
  A lonely gem surveys,
Astonished, doubly marks its beam,
  With art's most polished blaze.

Blest be the wild, sequestered shade,
  And blest the day and hour,
Where Peggy's charms I first surveyed,
  When first I felt their power!
The tyrant Death, with grim control,
  May seize my fleeting breath;
But tearing Peggy from my soul
  Must be a stronger death.

MY PEGGY'S FACE.

TUNE—*My Peggy's Face.*

MY Peggy's face, my Peggy's form,
The frost of hermit age might warm;
My Peggy's worth, my Peggy's mind,
Might charm the first of human kind.
I love my Peggy's angel air,
Her face so truly, heavenly fair,
Her native grace so void of art,
But I adore my Peggy's heart.

The lily's hue, the rose's dye,
The kindling lustre of an eye—
Who but owns their magic sway!
Who but knows they all decay!
The tender thrill, the pitying tear,
The generous purpose, nobly dear,
The gentle look, that rage disarms—
These are all immortal charms.

ADDRESS TO MR. WILLIAM TYTLER.

SENT WITH A SILHOUETTE PORTRAIT.

Revered defender of beauteous Stuart,[1]
Of Stuart, a name once respected —
A name which to love was the mark of a true heart,
But now 'tis despised and neglected.

Though something like moisture conglobes in my eye,
Let no one misdeem me disloyal;
A poor friendless wanderer may well claim a sigh,
Still more, if that wanderer were royal.

My fathers that name have revered on a throne;
My fathers have fallen to right it;
Those fathers would spurn their degenerate son,
That name should he scoffingly slight it.

Still in prayers for King George I most heartily join,
The Queen, and the rest of the gentry;
Be they wise, be they foolish, is nothing of mine,
Their title's avowed by my country.

[1] Mr. Tytler had published, in 1759, *An Inquiry, Historical and Critical, into the Evidence against Mary Queen of Scots.*

But why of that epocha make such a fuss,
  That gave us the Hanover stem?
If bringing them over was lucky for us,
  I'm sure 'twas as lucky for them.

But loyalty — truce! we're on dangerous ground!
  Who knows how the fashions may alter?
The doctrine to-day that is loyalty sound,
  To-morrow may bring us a halter!

I send you a trifle, a head of a bard,
  A trifle scarce worthy your care;
But accept it, good sir, as a mark of regard,
  Sincere as a saint's dying prayer.

Now life's chilly evening dim shades on your eye,
  And ushers the long dreary night;
But you, like the star that athwart gilds the sky,
  Your course to the latest is bright.

ON A YOUNG LADY

RESIDING ON THE BANKS OF THE SMALL RIVER DEVON, IN CLACKMANNANSHIRE, BUT WHOSE INFANT YEARS WERE SPENT IN AYRSHIRE.

Addressed to Miss Charlotte Hamilton, and intended for publication in Johnson's *Museum*. The tune was a beautiful Highland air, entitled *Bhanarach dhonn a chruidh*, or the *Pretty Milkmaid.*

How pleasant the banks of the clear winding Devon,
With green-spreading bushes, and flowers blooming fair!
But the bonniest flower on the banks of the Devon
Was once a sweet bud on the braes of the Ayr.

Mild be the sun on this sweet blushing flower,
In the gay rosy morn as it bathes in the dew,
And gentle the fall of the soft vernal shower,
That steals on the evening each leaf to renew!

Oh spare the dear blossom, ye orient breezes,
With chill hoary wing as ye usher the dawn!
And far be thou distant, thou reptile that seizes
The verdure and pride of the garden and lawn!

Let Bourbon exult in his gay-gilded lilies,
And England triumphant display her proud rose;
A fairer than either adorns the green valleys
Where Devon, sweet Devon, meandering flows.

ELEGY ON THE DEATH OF LORD PRESIDENT DUNDAS.

The Lord President of the Court of Session (Dundas) died on the 13th December, and it seems to have been suggested to Burns by Mr. Charles Hay, advocate, that he should bring his Muse into play for the celebration of the event. There must have been some reason beyond the merits of the President for Hay having advised this step, and for the proud soul of Burns having stooped to adopt it. He set to bewailing the decease of the great man in the usual style of the venal bards of the age of patronage, and, as might be expected, with no great success.

LONE on the bleaky hills the straying flocks
Shun the fierce storms among the sheltering rocks;
Down from the rivulets, red with dashing rains,
The gathering floods burst o'er the distant plains;
Beneath the blasts the leafless forests groan;
The hollow caves return a sullen moan.

Ye hills, ye plains, ye forests, and ye caves,
Ye howling winds, and wintry swelling waves,
Unheard, unseen, by human ear or eye,
Sad to your sympathetic scenes I fly;
Where to the whistling blast and water's roar

Pale Scotia's recent wound I may deplore.
Oh heavy loss, thy country ill could bear!
A loss these evil days can ne'er repair!

Justice, the high vicegerent of her God,
Her doubtful balance eyed, and swayed her
rod;
Hearing the tidings of the fatal blow
She sank, abandoned to the wildest wo.

Wrongs, injuries, from many a darksome den,
Now gay in hope explore the paths of men:
See from his cavern grim Oppression rise,
And throw on Poverty his cruel eyes;
Keen on the helpless victim see him fly,
And stifle, dark, the feebly-bursting cry.

Mark ruffian Violence, distained with crimes,
Rousing elate in these degenerate times;
View unsuspecting Innocence a prey,
As guileful Fraud points out the erring way:
While subtle Litigation's pliant tongue
The life-blood equal sucks of Right and Wrong:
Hark, injured Want recounts th' unlistened tale,
And much-wronged Misery pours th' unpitied
wail!

Ye dark waste hills, and brown unsightly plains,
To you I sing my grief-inspirèd strains:
Ye tempests, rage! ye turbid torrents, roll!

Ye suit the joyless tenor of my soul.
Life's social haunts and pleasures I resign,
Be nameless wilds and lonely wanderings mine,
To mourn the woes my country must endure,
That wound degenerate ages cannot cure.

A FAREWELL TO CLARINDA,

ON LEAVING EDINBURGH.

CLARINDA, mistress of my soul,
  The measured time is run!
The wretch beneath the dreary pole
  So marks his latest sun.

To what dark cave of frozen night
  Shall poor Sylvander hie,
Deprived of thee, his life and light,
  The sun of all his joy?

We part—but, by these precious drops
  That fill thy lovely eyes!
No other light shall guide my steps
  Till thy bright beams arise.

She, the fair sun of all her sex,
  Has blest my glorious day;
And shall a glimmering planet fix
  My worship to its ray?

CONTRIBUTIONS

TO THE SECOND VOLUME OF JOHNSON'S MUSEUM.[1]

WHISTLE AND I'LL COME TO YE, MY LAD.

Oh whistle and I'll come to ye, my lad,
Oh whistle and I'll come to ye, my lad;
Though father and mother and a' should gae
mad,
Oh whistle and I'll come to ye, my lad.

[1] The number of songs sent in Burns's handwriting to Johnson's *Scots Musical Museum* has been stated at one hundred and eighty; but many of these were old songs, gathered by him from oral tradition; many had only received from him a few improving touches; and only forty-seven were finally decided upon by Dr. Currie as wholly and undoubtedly the production of Burns. The poet himself, through the voluminousness of Johnson's collection seems to have disposed him to regard it as "the text-book and standard of Scottish song and music," felt ashamed of much that he had contributed to it. "Here, once for all," said he in a letter to Mr. Thomson, "let me apologise for the many silly compositions of mine in this work. Many beautiful airs wanted words, and in the hurry of other avocations, if I could string a parcel of rhymes together, anything near tolerable, I was fain to let them pass." On the other hand, a considerable number of his contributions to Johnson were equal to the best of his compositions, and had already attained popularity.

Come down the back stairs when ye come to
court me,
Come down the back stairs when ye come to
court me,
Come down the back stairs, and let naebody
see;
And come as ye were na coming to me.[1]

MACPHERSON'S FAREWELL.

TUNE — *M'Pherson's Rant.*

James Macpherson was a noted Highland freebooter, of uncommon personal strength, and an excellent performer on the violin. After holding the counties of Aberdeen, Banff, and Moray in fear for some years, he was seized by Duff of Braco, ancestor of the Earl of Fife, and tried before the sheriff of Banffshire (November 7, 1700), along with certain gypsies who had been taken in his company. In the prison, while he lay under sentence of death, he composed a song and an appropriate air, the former commencing thus: —

"I've spent my time in rioting,
Debauched my health and strength;
I squandered fast as pillage came,
And fell to shame at length.

1 Burns afterwards altered and extended this song.

But dantonly, and wantonly,
And rantingly I'll gae;
I'll play a tune, and dance it roun'
Beneath the gallows-tree."

When brought to the place of execution, on the Gallows-hill of Banff (Nov. 16), he played the tune on his violin, and then asked if any friend was present who would accept the instrument as a gift at his hands. No one coming forward, he indignantly broke the violin on his knee, and threw away the fragments; after which he submitted to his fate.

The verses of Burns—justly called by Mr. Lockhart "a grand lyric"—were designed as an improvement on those of the freebooter, preserving the same air.

FAREWELL, ye dungeons dark and strong,
The wretch's destinie!
Macpherson's time will not be long
On yonder gallows-tree.
Sae rantingly, sae wantonly,
Sae dauntingly gaed he;
He played a spring, and danced it round,
Below the gallows-tree.

Oh, what is Death but parting breath?
On many a bloody plain
I've dared his face, and in this place
I scorn him yet again!

Untie these bands from off my hands,
And bring to me my sword;

And there's no a man in all Scotlánd
But I'll brave him at a word.

I've lived a life of sturt and strife; turmoil
I die by treacherie:
It burns my heart I must depart,
And not avenged be.

Now farewell light, thou sunshine bright,
And all beneath the sky!
May coward shame distain his name,
The wretch that dares not die!

STAY, MY CHARMER.

Tune — *An Gille dubh ciar dhubh.*

Stay, my charmer, can you leave me?
Cruel, cruel to deceive me!
Well you know how much you grieve me;
Cruel charmer, can you go?
Cruel charmer, can you go?

By my love so ill requited,
By the faith you fondly plighted,
By the pangs of lovers slighted,
Do not, do not leave me so!
Do not, do not leave me so!

STRATHALLAN'S LAMENT.

The individual here meant is William, fourth Viscount of Strathallan, who fell on the insurgent side at the battle of Culloden, April, 1746. Burns, probably ignorant of his real fate, describes him as having survived the action, and taken refuge from the fury of the government forces in a Highland fastness.

THICKEST night, o'erhang my dwelling!
Howling tempests, o'er me rave!
Turbid torrents, wintry swelling,
Still surround my lonely cave![1]

Crystal streamlets gently flowing,
Busy haunts of base mankind,
Western breezes softly blowing,
Suit not my distracted mind.

In the cause of right engagèd,
Wrongs injurious to redress,

1 Variation in MS. in possession of Mr. B. Nightingale, Priory Road, London:—

"Thickest night, surround my dwelling!
Howling tempests, o'er me rave!
Turbid torrents, wintry swelling,
Roaring by my lonely cave!"

Honour's war we strongly wagèd,
  But the heavens denied success.

Ruin's wheel has driven o'er us,
  Not a hope that dare attend:
The wide world is all before us —
  But a world without a friend!

THE YOUNG HIGHLAND ROVER.

TUNE — *Morag.*

LOUD blaw the frosty breezes,
  The snaws the mountains cover;
Like winter on me seizes,
  Since my young Highland Rover [1]
  Far wanders nations over.
Where'er he go, where'er he stray,
  May Heaven be his warden,
Return him safe to fair Strathspey,
  And bonny Castle-Gordon!

The trees now naked groaning,
  Soon shall wi' leaves be hinging,

1 The Highland Rover is evidently meant for Prince Charles Stuart.

The birdies dowie moaning, sadly
Shall a' be blithely singing,
And every flower be springing.
Sae I'll rejoice the lee-lang day,
When by his mighty warden
My youth's returned to fair Strathspey,
And bonny Castle-Gordon.

RAVING WINDS AROUND HER BLOWING.

TUNE — *Macgregor of Ruara's Lament.*

" I composed these verses on Miss Isabella M'Leod of Raasay, alluding to her feelings on the death of her sister, and the still more melancholy death (1786) of her sister's husband, the late Earl of Loudon, who shot himself out of sheer heart-break at some mortifications he suffered owing to the deranged state of his finances." — *B.*

RAVING winds around her blowing,
Yellow leaves the woodlands strowing,
By a river hoarsely roaring,
Isabella strayed deploring:
" Farewell hours that late did measure
Sunshine days of joy and pleasure;
Hail, thou gloomy night of sorrow,
Cheerless night that knows no morrow!

"O'er the past too fondly wandering,
On the hopeless future pondering,
Chilly Grief my life-blood freezes,
Fell Despair my fancy seizes.
Life, thou soul of every blessing,
Load to Misery most distressing,
Gladly how would I resign thee,
And to dark oblivion join thee!"

MUSING ON THE ROARING OCEAN.

TUNE — *Druimion Dubh.*

"I composed these verses out of compliment to a Mrs. Maclachlan, whose husband is an officer in the East Indies." — *B.*

MUSING on the roaring ocean,
  Which divides my love and me,
Wearying Heaven in warm devotion,
  For his weal where'er he be;

Hope and Fear's alternate billow
  Yielding late to Nature's law,
Whisp'ring spirits round my pillow
  Talk of him that's far awa'.

Ye whom sorrow never wounded,
  Ye who never shed a tear,
Care-untroubled, joy-surrounded,
  Gaudy Day to you is dear.

Gentle Night, do thou befriend me,
  Downy Sleep, the curtain draw;
Spirits kind, again attend me,
  Talk of him that's far awa'!

BONNY PEGGY ALISON.

TUNE — *Braes o' Balquhidder.*

CHORUS.

I'LL kiss thee yet, yet,
  And I'll kiss thee o'er again,
And I'll kiss thee yet, yet,
  My bonny Peggy Alison!

Ilk care and fear, when thou art near,
  I ever mair defy them, O!
Young kings upon their hansel throne   newly-gained
  Are no sae blest as I am, O!

When in my arms, wi' a' thy charms,
  I clasp my countless treasure, O,

I seek nae mair o' heaven to share
  Than sic a moment's pleasure, O!

And by thy e'en, sae bonny blue,
  I swear I'm thine for ever, O!
And on thy lips I seal my vow,
  And break it shall I never, O![1]

TO CLARINDA,

WITH A PRESENT OF A PAIR OF DRINKING-GLASSES.

FAIR Empress of the Poet's soul,
  And Queen of Poetesses,
Clarinda, take this little boon,
  This humble pair of glasses.

And fill them high with generous juice,
  As generous as your mind,
And pledge me in the generous toast —
  "The whole of human kind!"

[1] Mr. William Douglas, whose expiscation of the mysterious story of Highland Mary entitles him to be heard with respect on any subject connected with Burns, is strongly of opinion that both *Mary Morison* and *Bonny Peggy Alison* refer to Ellison Begbie, the poet's early sweetheart, whose rejection of him just before his going to Irvine caused him so much discomfiture during that period of his life.

"To those who love us!" — second fill;
But not to those whom we love;
Lest we love those who love not us!
A third — "To thee and me, love!"

THE CHEVALIER'S LAMENT.

TUNE — *Captain O'Kean.*

The small birds rejoice in the green leaves returning,
The murmuring streamlet winds clear through the vale;
The hawthorn-trees blow in the dew of the morning,
And wild scattered cowslips bedeck the green dale:
But what can give pleasure, or what can seem fair,
While the lingering moments are numbered by care?
No flowers gaily springing, nor birds sweetly singing,
Can soothe the sad bosom of joyless despair.

The deed that I dared, could it merit their
malice,
A king and a father to place on his throne?
His right are these hills, and his right are these
valleys,
Where the wild beasts find shelter, but I can
find none.
But 'tis not my sufferings thus wretched, forlorn;
My brave gallant friends! 'tis your ruin I mourn;
Your deeds proved so loyal in hot bloody
trial —
Alas! I can make you no sweeter return!

EPISTLE TO HUGH PARKER.

Written from the farm of Ellisland, upon which Burns entered in June, 1788.

In this strange land, this uncouth clime,
A land unknown to prose or rhyme;
Where words ne'er crost the Muse's heckles,[1]
Nor limpet in poetic shackles;
A land that Prose did never view it,
Except when drunk he stacher't through it; staggered
Here, ambush'd by the chimla cheek, chimney

[1] Hackles — an instrument for dressing flax.

Hid in an atmosphere of reek, smoke
I hear a wheel thrum i' the neuk,
I hear it—for in vain I leuk.
The red peat gleams, a fiery kernel,
Enhusked by a fog infernal:
Here, for my wonted rhyming raptures,
I sit and count my sins by chapters.
For life and spunk like ither Christians,
I'm dwindled down to mere existence;
Wi' nae converse but Gallowa' bodies,[1]
Wi' nae kenn'd face but Jenny Geddes.[2]
Jenny, my Pegasean pride!
Dowie she saunters down Nithside, Sad
And aye a westlin leuk she throws,
While tears hap o'er her auld brown nose! cover
Was it for this, wi' canny care, gentle
Thou bure the Bard through many a shire?
At howes or hillocks never stumbled, hollows
And late or early never grumbled?
Oh, had I power like inclination,
I'd heeze thee up a constellation, raise
To canter with the Sagitarre,
Or loup the ecliptic like a bar;
Or turn the pole like any arrow;
Or, when auld Phœbus bids good-morrow,
Down the zodiac urge the race,
And cast dirt on his godship's face:

[1] Ellisland is near the borders of the stewartry of Kirkcudbright, a portion of the district popularly called Galloway.
[2] His mare.

For I could lay my bread and kail — broth
He'd ne'er cast saut upo' thy tail.
Wi' a' this care and a' this grief,
And sma', sma' prospect of relief,
And nought but peat-reek i' my head,
How can I write what ye can read?
Torbolton, twenty-fourth o' June,
Ye'll find me in a better tune;
But till we meet and weet our whistle,
Tak this excuse for nae epistle.

ROBERT BURNS.

I LOVE MY JEAN.

TUNE — *Miss Admiral Gordon's Strathspey.*

In the spring of 1788 Burns resolved to acknowledge Jean Armour as his wife. Until a proper house should be built at Ellisland she was to remain at Mauchline, with her only surviving child, Burns living in a mere hovel alone on his farm.

OF a' the airts the wind can blaw, — quarters
I dearly like the west,
For there the bonny lassie lives,
The lassie I lo'e best:

There's wild woods grow, and rivers row, roll
And monie a hill between; [1]
But day and night my fancy's flight
Is ever wi' my Jean.

I see her in the dewy flowers,
I see her sweet and fair;
I hear her in the tunefu' birds,
I hear her charm the air:

[1] The commencement of this stanza is given in Johnson's *Museum* —

"There wild woods grow," etc.,

as implying the nature of the scenery in the west. In Wood's *Songs of Scotland*, the reading is —

"Though wild woods grow, and rivers row,
Wi' monie a hill between,
Baith day and night," etc.,

evidently an alteration designed to improve the logic of the verse. It appears that both readings are wrong, for in the original manuscript of Burns's contributions to Johnson, in the possession of Archibald Hastie, Esq., the line is written: "There wild woods grow," etc., as in our text. Another example will serve to bring this peculiarity of composition more distinctly before the mind of the reader:

By Auchtertyre grows the aik,
On Yarrow banks the birken shaw;
But Phemie was a bonnier lass
Than braes o' Yarrow ever saw.

I have been reminded that the idea is not new in verse:

"ἐπειὴ μάλα πολλὰ μεταξὺ
Οὔρεά τε σκιόεντα, θάλασσά τε ἠχήεσσα."
Iliad, i. 156.

There's not a bonny flower that springs
  By fountain, shaw, or green,
There's not a bonny bird that sings,
  But minds me o' my Jean.[1]

[1] The first of these stanzas appeared in the third volume of Johnson's *Museum*. Burns's note upon it afterwards was: "This song I composed out of compliment to Mrs. Burns. *N. B.*—It was in the honeymoon." Two additional stanzas were some years afterwards produced by John Hamilton, music-seller in Edinburgh:

O blaw, ye westlin' winds, blaw saft,
  Amang the leafy trees,
Wi' balmy gale, frae hill and dale
  Bring hame the laden bees;
And bring the lassie back to me
  That's aye sae neat and clean;
Ae smile o' her wad banish care,
  Sae charming is my Jean.

What sighs and vows amang the knowes
  Hae passed atween us twa!
How fond to meet, how wae to part, sad
  That night she gaed awa'!
The powers aboon can only ken,
  To whom the heart is seen,
That nane can be sae dear to me
  As my sweet lovely Jean.

OH, WERE I ON PARNASSUS' HILL!

TUNE — *My Love is lost to me.*

We have to suppose the poet in his solitary life at Ellisland, gazing towards the hill of Corsincon, at the head of Nithsdale, beyond which, though at many miles' distance, was the valley in which his heart's idol lived.

OH, were I on Parnassus' hill,
Or had of Helicon my fill!
That I might catch poetic skill,
  To sing how dear I love thee.
But Nith maun be my Muse's well,
My Muse maun be thy bonny sel';[1]
On Corsincon I'll glower and spell, stare — discourse
  And write how dear I love thee.

Then come, sweet Muse, inspire my lay!
For a' the lee-lang simmer's day
I couldna sing, I couldna say,
  How much, how dear I love thee.

[1] An anonymous writer in the *Notes and Queries* points out a similar idea to this in Propertius (II. i. 3):

"Non hæc Calliope, non hæc mihi cantat Apollo,
Ingenium nobis ipsa puella facit."

I see thee dancing o'er the green,
Thy waist sae jimp, thy limbs sae clean,[1] slender
Thy tempting lips, thy roguish een —
By heaven and earth I love thee!

By night, by day, a-field, at hame,
The thoughts of thee my breast inflame;
And aye I muse and sing thy name —
I only live to love thee.
Though I were doomed to wander on
Beyond the sea, beyond the sun,
Till my last weary sand was run;
Till then — and then I love thee.[2]

VERSES IN FRIARS' CARSE HERMITAGE.

One piece of special good-fortune in Burns's situation at Ellisland was his having for his next neighbor, at less than a mile's distance along the bank of the Nith, Captain Riddell of Glenriddell, a man of literary and antiquarian spirit, and of kindly social nature. Captain Riddell had given Burns a key

[1] Clean in this relation means well-shaped — handsome.

[2] It is but four or five months since he said: "I admire you, I love you as a woman beyond any one in all the circle of creation. . . . . . I am yours, Clarinda, for life!"

admitting him to the grounds. On the 28th of June he composed, under the character of a bedesman, or alms-fed recluse, the following verses.

Thou whom chance may hither lead,
Be thou clad in russet weed,
Be thou decked in silken stole,
Grave these maxims on thy soul.
Life is but a day at most,
Sprung from night, in darkness lost;
Day, how rapid in its flight;
Day, how few must see the night.
Hope not sunshine every hour,
Fear not clouds will always lower.
Happiness is but a name,
Make content and ease thy aim.
Ambition is a meteor gleam;
Fame a restless, idle dream;
Pleasures, insects on the wing
Round Peace, the tenderest flower of Spring;
Those that sip the dew alone,
Make the butterflies thy own;
Those that would the bloom devour,
Crush the locusts — save the flower.
For the future be prepared,
Guard wherever thou canst guard;
But, thy utmost duly done,
Welcome what thou canst not shun.
Follies past, give thou to air,
Make their consequence thy care:

Keep the name of man in mind,
And dishonour not thy kind.
Reverence, with lowly heart,
Him whose wondrous work thou art;
Keep His goodness still in view,
Thy trust — and thy example too.

Stranger, go! Heaven be thy guide!
Quod the Bedesman on Nithside.

THE FÊTE CHAMPÊTRE.

TUNE — *Killiecrankie.*

According to the recital of Gilbert Burns: "When Mr. Cunninghame, of Enterkin, came to his estate, two mansion-houses on it, Enterkin and Anbank, were both in a ruinous state. Wishing to introduce himself with some *éclat* to the county, he got temporary erections made on the banks of Ayr, tastefully decorated with shrubs and flowers, for a supper and ball, to which most of the respectable families in the county were invited. It was a novelty, and attracted much notice. A dissolution of Parliament was soon expected, and this festivity was thought to be an introduction to a canvass for representing the county. Several other candidates were spoken of particularly Sir John Whitefoord, then residing at Cloncaird, commonly pronounced Glencaird, and Mr. Boswell, the well-known biographer of Dr. Johnson. The political views of this festive assemblage, which are alluded to in the ballad, if they ever existed, were, however, laid aside, as Mr. Cunninghame did not canvass the county." By the favor of W. Allasone Cunninghame, Esq., son of Mr. Cunninghame of Enterkin, I learn that this affair must have taken place in the summer of 1788.

Oh wha will to Saint Stephen's House,
To do our errands there, man?
Oh wha will to Saint Stephen's House,
O' th' merry lads o' Ayr, man?
Or will ye send a man-o'-law?
Or will ye send a sodger?
Or him wha led o'er Scotland a'
The meikle Ursa-Major?[1]

Come, will ye court a noble lord,
Or buy a score o' lairds, man?
For worth and honour pawn their word,
Their vote shall be Glencaird's, man.
Ane gies them coin, ane gies them wine,
Anither gies them clatter; idle stories
Anbank, wha guessed the ladies' taste,
He gies a Fête Champêtre.

[1] An allusion to the well-known joke of the elder Boswell, who, hearing his son speak of Johnson as a great luminary, quite a constellation, said: "Yes, *Ursa Major*."

When Love and Beauty heard the news,
  The gay greenwoods amang, man,
Where, gathering flowers and busking bowers,
  They heard the blackbird's sang, man,
A vow, they sealed it with a kiss,
  Sir Politics to fetter,
As theirs alone the patent-bliss
  To hold a Fête Champêtre.

Then mounted Mirth, on gleesome wing,
  Ower hill and dale she flew, man;
Ilk wimpling burn, ilk crystal spring, meandering
  Ilk glen and shaw she knew, man: wood
She summoned every social sprite,
  That sports by wood and water,
On th' bonny banks o' Ayr to meet,
  And keep this Fête Champêtre.

Cauld Boreas, wi' his boisterous crew,
  Were bound to stakes like kye, man;
And Cynthia's car, o' silver fu',
  Clamb up the starry sky, man:
Reflected beams dwell in the streams,
  Or down the current shatter;
The western breeze steals through the trees
  To view this Fête Champêtre.

How many a robe sae gaily floats,
  What sparkling jewels glance, man,
To Harmony's enchanting notes

As moves the mazy dance, man.
The echoing wood, the winding flood,
Like Paradise did glitter,
When angels met, at Adam's yett, gate
To hold their Fête Champêtre.

When Politics came there, to mix
And make his ether-stane, man![1]
He circled round the magic ground,
But entrance found he nane, man:
He blushed for shame, he quat his name, quit
Forswore it, every letter,
Wi' humble prayer to join and share
This festive Fête Champêtre.

THE DAY RETURNS.

TUNE — *Seventh of November.*

"Johnson's collection of Scots songs is going on in the third volume; and, of consequence, finds me a

[1] Alluding to a superstition, which represents adders as forming annually from their slough certain little annular stones of streaked coloring, which are occasionally found, and which are in reality beads fashioned and used by our early ancestors.

consumpt for a great deal of idle metre. One of the most tolerable things I have done in that way is two stanzas I made to an air a musical gentleman of my acquaintance [Captain Riddell, of Glenriddell] composed for the anniversary of his wedding-day, which happens on the 7th of November." — *Burns to Miss Chalmers, Sept.* 16, 1788.

THE day returns, my bosom burns,
  The blissful day we twa did meet;
Though winter wild in tempest toiled,
  Ne'er summer sun was half sae sweet.
Than a' the pride that loads the tide,
  And crosses o'er the sultry line,
Than kingly robes, than crowns and globes,
  Heaven gave me more — it made thee mine!

While day and night can bring delight,
  Or Nature aught of pleasure give,
While joys above my mind can move,
  For thee, and thee alone, I live.
When that grim foe of life below
  Comes in between to make us part,
The iron hand that breaks our band,
  It breaks my bliss — it breaks my heart!

FIRST EPISTLE TO MR. GRAHAM OF FINTRY.

Burns had been told by some of his literary friends, that it was a great error to write in Scotch, seeing that thereby he was cut off from the appreciation of the English public. He was disposed to give way to this hint, and henceforth to compose chiefly in English, or at least to try his hand upon the soft lyres of Twickenham and Richmond, in the hope of succeeding equally well as he had hitherto done upon the rustic reed of Scotland. It seems to have been a great mistake. The flow of versification and the felicity of diction, for which Burns's Scottish poems and songs are remarkable, vanish when he attempts the southern strain. We see this well exemplified in a poem of the present summer, in which he aimed at the style of Pope's *Moral Epistles*, while at the same time he sought to advance his personal fortunes through the medium of a patron.

WHEN Nature her great master-piece designed,
And framed her last, best work, the human mind,
Her eye intent on all the mazy plan,
She formed of various parts the various man.

Then first she calls the useful many forth,
Plain plodding industry, and sober worth ;

Thence peasants, farmers, native sons of earth,
And merchandise' whole genus take their birth;
Each prudent cit a warm existence finds,
And all mechanics' many-apron'd kinds.
Some other rarer sorts are wanted yet,
The lead and buoy are needful to the net;
The *caput mortuum* of gross desires
Makes a material for mere knights and squires;
The martial phosphorus is taught to flow;
She kneads the lumpish philosophic dough,
Then marks the unyielding mass with grave designs,
Law, physic, politics, and deep divines;
Last, she sublimes the Aurora of the poles,
The flashing elements of female souls.
The order'd system fair before her stood,
Nature, well pleased, pronounced it very good;
But ere she gave creating labour o'er,
Half-jest, she tried one curious labour more.
Some spumy, fiery, *ignis fatuus* matter,
Such as the slightest breath of air might scatter;
With arch alacrity and conscious glee
(Nature may have her whim as well as we,
Her Hogarth-art perhaps she meant to shew it),
She forms the thing, and christens it — a Poet;
Creature, though oft the prey of care and sorrow,
When blest to-day, unmindful of to-morrow;
A being formed t' amuse his graver friends,
Admired and praised — and there the homage ends:

A mortal quite unfit for Fortune's strife,
Yet oft the sport of all the ills of life;
Prone to enjoy each pleasure riches give,
Yet haply wanting wherewithal to live;
Longing to wipe each tear, to heal each groan,
Yet frequent all unheeded in his own.
But honest Nature is not quite a Turk;
She laughed at first, then felt for her poor work.
Pitying the propless climber of mankind,
She cast about a standard tree to find;
And, to support his helpless woodbine state,
Attached him to the generous truly great,
A title, and the only one I claim,
To lay strong hold for help on bounteous Graham.

Pity the tuneful Muses' hapless train,
Weak, timid landsmen on life's stormy main!
Their hearts no selfish stern absorbent stuff,
That never gives — though humbly takes enough;
The little fate allows, they share as soon,
Unlike sage proverb'd wisdom's hard-wrung boon.
The world were blest did bliss on them depend:
Ah, that "the friendly e'er should want a friend!"
Let prudence number o'er each sturdy son,
Who life and wisdom at one race begun,

Who feel by reason and who give by rule
(Instinct's a brute, and sentiment a fool!) —
Who make poor *will do* wait upon *I should* —
We own they're prudent, but who feels they're good?
Ye wise ones, hence! ye hurt the social eye!
God's image rudely etched on base alloy!
But come, ye who the godlike pleasure know,
Heaven's attribute distinguished — to bestow!
Whose arms of love would grasp the human race:
Come thou who giv'st with all a courtier's grace,
Friend of my life, true patron of my rhymes,
Prop of my dearest hopes for future times!
Why shrinks my soul half-blushing, half-afraid,
Backward, abashed, to ask thy friendly aid?
I know my need, I know thy giving hand,
I crave thy friendship at thy kind command;
But there are such who court the tuneful Nine —
Heavens! should the branded character be mine! —
Whose verse in manhood's pride sublimely flows,
Yet vilest reptiles in their begging prose.
Mark, how their lofty independent spirit
Soars on the spurning wing of injured merit!
Seek not the proofs in private life to find;
Pity the best of words should be but wind!

So to heaven's gate the lark's shrill song ascends,
But grovelling on the earth the carol ends.
In all the clam'rous cry of starving want,
They dun benevolence with shameless front;
Oblige them, patronise their tinsel lays,
They persecute you all your future days!
Ere my poor soul such deep damnation stain,
My horny fist assume the plough again;
The piebald jacket let me patch once more;
On eighteenpence a week I've lived before.
Though, thanks to Heaven, I dare even that last shift!
I trust, meantime, my boon is in thy gift:
That, placed by thee upon the wished-for height,
Where, man and nature fairer in her sight,
My Muse may imp her wing for some sublimer flight.

MRS. FERGUSSON OF CRAIGDARROCH'S LAMENTATION FOR THE DEATH OF HER SON,

AN UNCOMMONLY PROMISING YOUTH OF EIGHTEEN OR NINETEEN YEARS OF AGE.

"I am just arrived from Nithsdale, and will be here a fortnight. I was on horseback this morning by three o'clock; for between my wife and my farm is just forty-six miles. As I jogged on in the dark, I was taken with a poetic fit as follows." — *Burns to Mrs. Dunlop*, 27*th Sept.* 1788.

FATE gave the word, the arrow sped,
  And pierced my darling's heart;
And with him all the joys are fled
  Life can to me impart.
By cruel hands the sapling drops,
  In dust dishonoured laid:
So fell the pride of all my hopes,
  My age's future shade.

The mother linnet in the brake
  Bewails her ravished young;
So I, for my lost darling's sake,
  Lament the live-day long.
Death! oft I've feared thy fatal blow,
  Now, fond I bare my breast;
Oh, do thou kindly lay me low
  With him I love, at rest![1]

[1] It is a curious circumstance regarding the brief poem conveyed by this letter, that a copy of it in the possession of Mr. Allason Cunninghame of Logan House, Ayrshire, is understood by that gentleman's family to have been sent to his grandmother, Burns's early patron, Mrs. General Stewart of Afton, as a deploration of the death of her only son, Alexander Gordon Stewart, who died at a military academy at Strasburg, the 5th December, 1787. Allan Cunningham speaks of a copy of the poem in his possession bearing a note by the author, which shows that he really had endeavored to turn this piece to the account of gratifying two friends. "*The*

THE LAZY MIST.

TUNE—*The Lazy Mist.*

THE lazy mist hangs from the brow of the hill,
Concealing the course of the dark-winding rill;
How languid the scenes, late so sprightly, appear!
As Autumn to Winter resigns the pale year.
The forests are leafless, the meadows are brown,
And all the gay foppery of Summer is flown:
Apart let me wander, apart let me muse,
How quick Time is flying, how keen Fate pursues!

Mother's Lament," he says, "was composed partly with a view to Mrs. Fergusson of Craigdarroch, and partly to the worthy patroness of my early muse, Mrs. Stewart of Afton." We may suppose that the parity of the two cases, and their nearness in point of time, had produced but one indivisible impression in the mind of the bard. Yet there is reason to believe that, in his complaisance towards his friends, he was somewhat over-eager to gratify them with poetical compliments, and oftener than once caused one to pay a double debt. We shall find that the little poem beginning, *Sensibility, how charming*, was first written on certain experiences of Mrs. M'Lehose, and sent to her, but afterwards addressed to "my dear and much-honoured friend, Mrs. Dunlop." So the reader will perceive that even Burns had his little *mystères d'atelier.*

How long I have lived — but how much lived in vain!
How little of life's scanty span may remain!
What aspects Old Time, in his progress, has worn!
What ties cruel Fate in my bosom has torn!
How foolish, or worse, till our summit is gained!
And downward, how weakened, how darkened, how pained!
This life's not worth having with all it can give:
For something beyond it poor man sure must live.

I HAE A WIFE O' MY AIN.

We may well believe that it was a time of great happiness to Burns when he first saw his mistress installed in her little mansion, and felt himself the master of a household, however humble — looked up to by a wife as "the goodman," and by a host of dependants as "the master." His sentiments on this occasion were in part expressed by the following vigorous and characteristic, though not very delicate verses. They are in imitation of an old ballad.

I HAE a wife o' my ain,
  I'll partake wi' naebody;

I'll tak cuckold frae nane,
  I'll gie cuckold to naebody.

I hae a penny to spend,
  There — thanks to naebody;
I hae naething to lend,
  I'll borrow frae naebody.

I am naebody's lord,
  I'll be slave to naebody;
I hae a guid braid sword,
  I'll tak dunts frae naebody. blows

I'll be merry and free,
  I'll be sad for naebody;
If naebody care for me,
  I'll care for naebody.

AULD LANG SYNE.

SHOULD auld acquaintance be forgot,
  And never brought to mind?
Should auld acquaintance be forgot,
  And days o' lang syne?

CHORUS.

For auld lang syne, my dear,
  For auld lang syne,

We'll tak a cup o' kindness yet
For auld lang syne.

We twa hae run about the braes,
And pu'd the gowans fine; daisies
But we've wandered monie a weary foot,
Sin' auld lang syne.

We twa hae paidl't i' the burn,
Frae morning sun till dine;
But seas between us braid hae roared,
Sin' auld lang syne.

And here's a hand, my trusty fiere companion
And gie's a hand o' thine;
And we'll tak a right guid willie-waught, hearty pull
For auld lang syne.

And surely you'll be your pint-stoup, flagon
And surely I'll be mine;
And we'll tak a cup o' kindness yet
For auld lang syne.[1]

[1] Burns came to indulge in little mystifications respecting his songs. Though in a letter to Mrs. Dunlop he speaks of *Auld Lang Syne* as an old fragment, and afterwards communicated it to George Thomson, with an expression of self-congratulation on having been so fortunate as to recover it from an old man's singing, the second and third verses — those expressing the recollections of youth, and certainly the finest of the set — are by himself. So also of *Go fetch to me a pint of wine*, he afterwards acknowledged that only the first

MY BONNY MARY.

Go fetch to me a pint o' wine,
And fill it in a silver tassie; cup
That I may drink before I go,
A service to my bonny lassie.
The boat rocks at the pier o' Leith,
Fu' loud the wind blaws frae the Ferry;
The ship rides by the Berwick-Law,[1]
And I maun leave my bonny Mary.

The trumpets sound, the banners fly,
The glittering spears are rankèd ready;

verse (four lines) was old, the rest his own. The old verse was probably the same with one which occurs near the close of a homely ballad, printed in Hogg and Motherwell's edition of Burns, as preserved by Mr. Peter Buchan, who further communicates that the ballad was composed in 1636, by Alexander Lesly of Edin, on Doveran side, grandfather to the celebrated Archbishop Sharpe:—

"Ye'll bring me here a pint of wine,
A server and a silver tassie,
That I may drink, before I gang,
A health to my ain bonny lassie."

1 North Berwick-Law, a conical hill near the shore of the Firth of Forth, very conspicuous at Edinburgh, from which it is distant about twenty miles.

The shouts o' war are heard afar,
  The battle closes thick and bloody.
But it's not the roar o' sea or shore
  Wad make me langer wish to tarry;
Nor shouts o' war that's heard afar —
  It's leaving thee, my bonny Mary.

LINES WRITTEN IN FRIARS' CARSE HERMITAGE.

Extended Copy.

THOU whom chance may hither lead,
Be thou clad in russet weed,
Be thou deckt in silken stole,
Grave these counsels on thy soul.

Life is but a day at most,
Sprung from night, in darkness lost; [1]
Hope not sunshine every hour,
Fear not clouds will always lower.

[1] In the shorter copy, an additional couplet is here inserted —

Day, how rapid in its flight!
Day, how few must see the night!

As Youth and Love with sprightly dance,
Beneath thy morning-star advance,
Pleasure with her siren air
May delude the thoughtless pair;
Let Prudence bless Enjoyment's cup,
Then raptured sip, and sip it up.

As thy day grows warm and high,
Life's meridian flaming nigh,
Dost thou spurn the humble vale?
Life's proud summits wouldst thou scale?
Check thy climbing step, elate,
Evils lurk in felon wait:
Dangers, eagle-pinioned, bold,
Soar around each cliffy hold,
While cheerful peace, with linnet song,
Chants the lowly dells among.

As the shades of evening close,
Beck'ning thee to long repose,
As life itself becomes disease,
Seek the chimney-nook of ease:
There ruminate with sober thought,
On all thou'st seen, and heard, and wrought,
And teach the sportive younkers round,
Saws of experience, sage and sound.
Say, man's true genuine estimate,
The grand criterion of his fate,
Is not — art thou high or low?

Did thy fortune ebb or flow?[1]
Did many talents gild thy span?
Or frugal Nature grudge thee one?
Tell them, and press it on their mind,
As thou thyself must shortly find,
The smile or frown of awful Heaven
To virtue or to vice is given.
Say, to be just, and kind, and wise,
There solid self-enjoyment lies;
That foolish, selfish, faithless ways
Lead to be wretched, vile, and base.

Thus resigned and quiet, creep
To the bed of lasting sleep;
Sleep, whence thou shalt ne'er awake,
Night, where dawn shall never break,
Till future life, future no more,
To light and joy the good restore,
To light and joy unknown before.

Stranger, go! Heaven be thy guide!
Quod the Bedesman of Nithside![2]

[1] Variation —

Say, man's true genuine estimate
The grand criterion of their fate,
The important query of their state,
Is not — art thou high or low?
Did thy fortune ebb or flow?
Wast thou cottager or king,
Peer or peasant? — no such thing!
Did many talents, etc.

[2] This extended copy of the lines for Friars' Carse Hermit-

ELEGY ON THE YEAR 1788.

Jan. 1, 1789.

For Lords or Kings I dinna mourn,
E'en let them die — for that they're born:
But oh! prodigious to reflec'!
A towmont, sirs, is gane to wreck! twelvemonth
Oh Eighty-eight, in thy sma' space
What dire events hae taken place!
Of what enjoyments thou hast reft us!
In what a pickle thou hast left us!

The Spanish empire's tint a head,[1] lost
And my auld teethless Bawtie's [2] dead;
The tulzie's sair 'tween Pitt and Fox, fight
And our guidwife's wee birdie cocks:
The tane is game, a bluidie devil,
But to the hen-birds unco civil;
The tither's something dour o' treadin', unsparing
But better stuff ne'er clawed a midden. dunghill

age was produced in December. We agree with Allan Cunningham in seeing in this second effort a proof of the comparative labor which Burns encountered in attempting to compose in pure English. The restricted religious views of the poet will be remarked.

[1] Charles III., king of Spain, died on the 13th of December, 1788.

[2] A generic familiar name for a dog in Scotland.

Ye ministers, come mount the pu'pit,
And cry till ye be hearse and roopit hoarse — raucous
For Eighty-eight he wished you weel,
And gied ye a' baith gear and meal; money
E'en monie a plack, and monie a peck, coin
Ye ken yoursel's, for little feck! . . . consideration
Observe the very nowt and sheep, cattle
How dowf and dowie now they creep: dull — sad
Nay, even the yirth itsel' does cry,
For Embro' wells are grutten dry.[1] Edinburgh — wept

Oh Eighty-nine, thou's but a bairn,
And no owre auld, I hope, to learn!
Thou beardless boy, I pray tak care,
Thou now has got thy daddy's chair,
Nae hand-cuffed, muzzled, hap-shackled foot-tied
Regent,[2]
But, like himsel', a full free agent.
Be sure ye follow out the plan
Nae waur than he did, honest man!
As muckle better as you can.

1 The Edinburgh newspapers of this period contain many references to a scarcity of water, in consequence of severe frost.

2 The king having shown symptoms of unsound mind in November, the public was at this time agitated with discussions as to the choice of a regent.

A SKETCH.

Burns meditated a laborious poem, to be entitled *The Poet's Progress*, probably of an autobiographical nature. He submitted to Mr. Stewart various short pieces designed to form part of this poem, but none have been preserved except the following.[1]

A LITTLE, upright, pert, tart, tripping wight,
And still his precious self his dear delight;
Who loves his own smart shadow in the streets,
Better than e'er the fairest she he meets.
A man of fashion, too, he made his tour,
Learned *vive la bagatelle, et vive l'amour;*
So travelled monkeys their grimace improve,
Polish their grin, nay, sigh for ladies' love.
Much specious lore, but little understood;
Veneering oft outshines the solid wood:
His solid sense — by inches you must tell,
But mete his cunning by the old Scotch ell;
His meddling vanity, a busy fiend,
Still making work his selfish craft must mend.[2]

[1] It is not unlikely that the lines on William Smellie, already introduced, were intended to form a part of *The Poet's Progress.*

[2] It is painful to come to the conclusion, from a remark and quotation in a subsequent letter, that this selfish, superficial wight was — Creech — the same "Willie" whom Burns de-

EXTEMPORE TO CAPTAIN RIDDEL,

ON RETURNING A NEWSPAPER.

On returning a newspaper which Captain Riddel had sent to him for his perusal, containing some strictures on his poetry, Burns added a note in impromptu verse.

ELLISLAND, *Monday Evening.*

YOUR news and review, sir, I've read through and through, sir,
With little admiring or blaming;
The papers are barren of home-news or foreign,
No murders or rapes worth the naming.

Our friends, the reviewers, those chippers and hewers,
Are judges of mortar and stone, sir;
But of *meet* or *unmeet*, in a *fabric complete*,
I'll boldly pronounce they are none, sir.

My goose-quill too rude is to tell all your goodness
Bestowed on your servant the poet;
Would to God I had one like a beam of the sun,
And then all the world, sir, should know it!

scribed in such affectionate terms in May, 1787, and to whom he then wished "a pow as auld's Methusalem."

ODE:

SACRED TO THE MEMORY OF MRS. OSWALD.

The irritable genius of Burns led him often to view persons and things very much as they affected himself. The same lord, gentleman, or lady, who, receiving him with urbanity, became the theme of his kindest feelings, might have come in for the eternal stigma of his satire, if, by a slight change of circumstances, he or she had been a cause of personal annoyance to him, or awakened his jealous apprehensions regarding his own dignity. In the course of the present month, an example of this infirmity of temper occurs. Let himself be the recorder of the incident, it being premised that the lady whom he thus holds up to execration was one fairly liable to no such censure!

"In January last, on my road to Ayrshire, I had to put up at Bailie Whigham's in Sanquhar, the only tolerable inn in the place. The frost was keen, and the grim evening and howling wind were ushering in a night of snow and drift. My horse and I were both much fatigued with the labours of the day; and just as my friend the bailie and I were bidding defiance to the storm, over a smoking bowl, in wheels the funeral pageantry of the late Mrs. Oswald, and poor I am forced to brave all the terrors of the tempestuous night, and jade my horse — my young favourite horse, whom I had just christened Pegasus

— further on through the wildest hills and moors of Ayrshire to the next inn! The powers of poetry and prose sink under me when I would describe what I felt. Suffice it to say, that when a good fire at New Cumnock had so far recovered my frozen sinews, I sat down and wrote the enclosed ode."

DWELLER in yon dungeon dark,
Hangman of creation, mark!
Who in widow-weeds appears,
Laden with unhonoured years,
Noosing with care a bursting purse,
Baited with many a deadly curse!

STROPHE.

View the withered beldam's face —
Can thy keen inspection trace
Aught of humanity's sweet melting grace?
Note that eye, 'tis rheum o'erflows,
Pity's flood there never rose.
See these hands, ne'er stretched to save,
Hands that took — but never gave.
Keeper of Mammon's iron chest,
Lo! there she goes, unpitied and unblest
She goes, but not to realms of everlasting rest!

ANTISTROPHE.

Plunderer of armies, lift thine eyes
(A while forbear, ye tort'ring fiends);
Seest thou whose step, unwilling, hither bends?

No fallen angel, hurled from upper skies;
'Tis thy trusty quondam mate,
Doomed to share thy fiery fate,
She, tardy, hellward plies.

EPODE.

And are they of no more avail,
Ten thousand glittering pounds a year?
In other words, can Mammon fail,
Omnipotent as he is here?
O bitter mockery of the pompous bier,
While down the wretched vital part is driv'n!
The cave-lodged beggar, with a conscience clear,
Expires in rags, unknown, and goes to heav'n.

TO JOHN TAYLOR.

Burns had arrived at Wanlockhead on a winter day, when the roads were slippery with ice, and the blacksmith of the place, busied with other pressing matters in the forge, could not spare time for *frosting* the shoes of the poet's mare. Burns called for pen and ink, and wrote these verses to John Taylor, a person of influence in Wanlockhead, on the receipt of which, Taylor spoke to the smith, and the smith flew to his tools, and sharpened the horse's shoes.

WITH Pegasus upon a day,
Apollo weary flying,

(Through frosty hills the journey lay,)
  On foot the way was plying.

Poor slipshod giddy Pegasus
  Was but a sorry walker;
To Vulcan then Apollo goes,
  To get a frosty calker.

Obliging Vulcan fell to work,
  Threw by his coat and bonnet,
And did Sol's business in a crack;
  Sol paid him with a sonnet.

Ye Vulcan's sons of Wanlockhead,
  Pity my sad disaster;
My Pegasus is poorly shod —
  I'll pay you like my master.

RAMAGE'S, 3 *o'clock.*

SKETCH:

INSCRIBED TO CHARLES JAMES FOX.

How Wisdom and Folly meet, mix, and unite;
How Virtue and Vice blend their black and their
    white;
How Genius, the illustrious father of Fiction,
Confounds Rule and Law, reconciles Contradic-
    tion —

I sing: if these mortals, the critics, should bustle,
I care not, not I; let the critics go whistle.

But now for a Patron, whose name and whose glory
At once may illustrate and honour my story.

Thou first of our orators, first of our wits,
Yet whose parts and acquirements seem mere lucky hits;
With knowledge so vast, and with judgment so strong,
No man with the half of 'em e'er went far wrong;
With passions so potent, and fancies so bright,
No man with the half of 'em e'er went quite right;
A sorry, poor misbegot son of the Muses,
For using thy name offers fifty excuses.[1]

[Good L—d, what is man? for as simple he looks,
Do but try to develop his hooks and his crooks;
With his depths and his shallows, his good and his evil,
All in all he's a problem must puzzle the devil.

[1] The verses following within brackets were added afterwards.

On his one ruling passion Sir Pope hugely labours,
That, like th' old Hebrew walking-switch, eats up its neighbours:
Mankind are his show-box — a friend, would you know him?
Pull the string, ruling passion the picture will shew him.
What pity, in rearing so beauteous a system,
One trifling particular, Truth, should have missed him;
For, spite of his fine theoretic positions,
Mankind is a science defies definitions.

Some sort all our qualities each to its tribe,
And think human nature they truly describe;
Have you found this or t'other! there's more in the wind,
As by one drunken fellow his comrades you'll find.
But such is the flaw, or the depth of the plan,
In the make of that wonderful creature called Man,
No two virtues, whatever relation they claim,
Nor even two different shades of the same,
Though like as was ever twin-brother to brother,
Possessing the one shall imply you've the óther.[1]

[1] The verses following this line were first printed from a manuscript of Burns, in Pickering's edition.

But truce with abstraction, and truce with the
Muse,
Whose rhymes you'll perhaps, sir, ne'er deign
to peruse:
Will you leave your justings, your jars, and
your quarrels,
Contending with Billy for proud-nodding laurels?
My much-honoured Patron, believe your poor
Poet,
Your courage much more than your prudence
you shew it.
In vain with Squire Billy for laurels you
struggle,
He'll have them by fair trade, if not he will
smuggle;
Not cabinets even of kings would conceal 'em,
He'd up the back-stairs, and by G— he would
steal 'em!
Then feats like Squire Billy's you ne'er can
achieve 'em:
It is not, out-do him — the task is, out-thieve
him!]

4th April, 1789.

ON A WOUNDED HARE.

"One morning lately, as I was out pretty early in the fields, sowing some grass-seeds, I heard the burst of a shot from a neighbouring plantation, and presently a poor little wounded hare came crippling by me. You will guess my indignation at the inhuman fellow who could shoot a hare at this season, when all of them have young ones."—*Burns to Mr. Cunningham*, 4*th May*, 1789.

INHUMAN man! curse on thy barbarous art,
And blasted be thy murder-aiming eye!
May never pity soothe thee with a sigh,
Nor ever pleasure glad thy cruel heart!

Go live, poor wanderer of the wood and field,
The bitter little that of life remains:
No more the thickening brakes or verdant plains
To thee a home, or food, or pastime yield.

Seek, mangled innocent, some wonted form;
That wonted form, alas! thy dying bed!
The sheltering rushes whistling o'er thy head,
The cold earth with thy blood-stained bosom warm.

Perhaps a mother's anguish adds its wo;
The playful pair crowd fondly by thy side;
Ah! helpless nurslings, who will now provide
That life a mother only can bestow?

Oft as by winding Nith I, musing, wait
The sober eve, or hail the cheerful dawn,
I'll miss thee sporting o'er the dewy lawn,
And curse the ruthless wretch, and mourn thy hapless fate.

DELIA.

There is usually printed in Burns's works a little ode, entitled *Delia*, which, from its deficiency of force and true feeling, some have suspected to be not his composition. Allan Cunningham tells a feasible-enough-looking story regarding it. "One day, when the poet was at Brownhill, in Nithsdale, a friend read some verses composed after the pattern of Pope's song by a person of quality, and said: 'Burns, this is beyond you. The Muse of Kyle cannot match the Muse of London city.' The poet took the paper, hummed the verses over, and then recited *Delia, an Ode.*" There is not anything in this anecdote inconsistent with the fact, that Burns sent the ode for insertion in a London newspaper. (?)

"MR. PRINTER — If the productions of a simple ploughman can merit a place in the same paper with Sylvester Otway, and the other favourites of the Muses who illuminate the *Star* with the lustre of genius, your insertion of the enclosed trifle will be succeeded by future communications from yours, &c.

"R. BURNS.

"ELLISLAND, *near Dumfries*,
18*th May*, 1789."

FAIR the face of orient day,
Fair the tints of op'ning rose;
But fairer still my Delia dawns,
More lovely far her beauty shews.

Sweet the lark's wild warbled lay,
Sweet the tinkling rill to hear;
But, Delia, more delightful still,
Steal thine accents on mine ear.

The flower-enamoured busy bee
The rosy banquet loves to sip;
Sweet the streamlet's limpid lapse
To the sun-browned Arab's lip.

But, Delia, on thy balmy lips
Let me, no vagrant insect, rove;
O let me steal one liquid kiss,
For, oh! my soul is parched with love!

ON SEEING A WOUNDED HARE LIMP BY ME,

WHICH A FELLOW HAD JUST SHOT.

The poem on the Hare had been sent to Dr. Gregory of Edinburgh, for whose critical judgment and general character Burns entertained a high veneration. Dr. Gregory's criticisms led to certain alterations, the result of which was as follows.

INHUMAN man! curse on thy barbarous art,
And blasted be thy murder-aiming eye;
May never pity soothe thee with a sigh,
Nor ever pleasure glad thy cruel heart!

Go live, poor wanderer of the wood and field!
The bitter little that of life remains:
No more the thickening brakes and verdant plains
To thee shall home, or food, or pastime yield.

Seek, mangled wretch, some place of wonted rest,
No more of rest, but now thy dying bed!
The sheltering rushes whistling o'er thy head,
The cold earth with thy bloody bosom prest.

Oft as by winding Nith I, musing, wait
 The sober eve, or hail the cheerful dawn,
 I'll miss thee sporting o'er the dewy lawn,
And curse the ruffian's aim, and mourn thy
 hapless fate.

LETTER TO JAMES TENNANT, OF GLENCONNER.[1]

Auld comrade dear, and brither sinner,
How's a' the folk about Glenconner?
How do you, this blae eastlin wind, blue
That's like to blaw a body blind?
For me, my faculties are frozen,
And ilka member nearly dozen'd. stupefied
I've sent you here, by Johnnie Simson,
Twa sage philosophers to glimpse on:
Smith, wi' his sympathetic feeling,
And Reid, to common-sense appealing.
Philosophers have fought and wrangled,
And meikle Greek and Latin mangled,
Till, wi' their logic jargon tir'd,
And in the depth of science mir'd,
To common-sense they now appeal,
What wives and wabsters see and feel. weavers

[1] An old friend of the poet and his family, who assisted him in his choice of the farm of Ellisland.

But, hark ye, friend! I charge you strictly,
Peruse them, and return them quickly,
For now I'm grown sae cursed douce, wise
I pray and ponder butt the house; in the outer room
My shins, my lane, I there sit roastin',
Perusing Bunyan, Brown, and Boston:
Till by and by, if I haud on, hold
I'll grunt a real gospel groan.
Already I begin to try it,
To cast my e'en up like a pyet, magpie
When by the gun she tumbles o'er,
Flutt'ring and gasping in her gore:
Sae shortly you shall see me bright,
A burning and a shining light.

My heart-warm love to guid auld Glen,
The ace and wale o' honest men. choice
When bending down wi' auld gray hairs,
Beneath the load of years and cares,
May He who made him still support him,
And views beyond the grave comfórt him;
His worthy fam'ly far and near,
God bless them a' wi' grace and gear! goods

My auld school-fellow, Preacher Willie,
The manly tar, my Mason billie, comrade
And Auchenbay, I wish him joy;
If he's a parent, lass or boy,
May he be dad, and Meg the mither,
Just five-and-forty years thegither!

And no forgetting Wabster Charlie,
I'm told he offers very fairly.
And, Lord, remember Singing Sannock
Wi' hale breeks, saxpence, and a bannock;[1] cake
And next my auld acquaintance Nancy,
Since she is fitted to her fancy;
And her kind stars hae airted till her directed
A good chiel wi' a pickle siller. small quantity
My kindest, best respects I sen' it,
To Cousin Kate and Sister Janet;
Tell them, frae me, wi' chiels be cautious, lads
For, faith, they'll aiblins fin' them possibly
fashious. troublesome
And lastly, Jamie, for yoursel',
May guardian angels tak a spell,
And steer you seven miles south o' hell.
But first, before you see heaven's glory,
May ye get monie a merry story;
Monie a laugh, and monie a drink,
And aye eneugh o' needfu' clink. money

Now fare ye weel, and joy be wi' you;
For my sake this I beg it o' you,
Assist poor Simson a' ye can,
Ye'll fin' him just an honest man:
Sae I conclude, and quat my chanter,
Yours, saint or sinner,

ROB THE RANTER.

[1] "Fortune, if thou 'll but gie me still
Hale breeks, a scone, and whisky gill," etc.
Scotch Drink.

ADDRESS TO THE TOOTHACHE.

My curse upon thy venomed stang, sting
That shoots my tortured gums alang;
And through my lugs gies monie a twang, ears
Wi' gnawing vengeance,
Tearing my nerves wi' bitter pang,
Like racking engines!

When fevers burn, or ague freezes,
Rheumatics gnaw, or cholic squeezes,
Our neighbour's sympathy may ease us
Wi' pitying moan;
But thee — thou hell o' a' diseases,
Aye mocks our groan!

Adown my beard the slavers trickle!
I kick the wee stools o'er the mickle,
As round the fire the giglets mocking children
keckle, laugh
To see me loup; jump
While, raving mad, I wish a heckle flax-comb
Were in their doup. backside

O' a' the num'rous human dools, sorrows
Ill har'sts, daft bargains, cutty-stools, foolish

Or worthy friends raked i' the mools, clods
Sad sight to see!
The tricks o' knaves, or fash o' fools — trouble
Thou bear'st the gree. superiority

Where'er that place be priests ca' hell,
Whence a' the tones o' misery yell,
And rankèd plagues their numbers tell,
In dreadfu' raw, row, order
Thou, Toothache, surely bear'st the bell
Amang them a'!

O thou grim mischief-making chiel,
That gars the notes of discord squeel,
Till daft Mankind aft dance a reel
In gore a shoe-thick! —
Gie a' the faes o' Scotland's weal
A towmond's toothache! twelvemonth

THE KIRK'S ALARM.

Dr. William M'Gill, one of the two ministers conjoined in the parochial charge of Ayr, had published in 1786, *A Practical Essay on the Death of Jesus Christ, in Two Parts; containing,* 1, *the History,* 2, *the Doctrine of his Death,* which was supposed to inculcate principles of both Arian and Socinian character, and provoked many severe censures from the more rigid party of the church. M'Gill remained silent under the attacks of his opponents, till Dr. William Peebles of Newton-upon-Ayr, a neighbor, and hitherto a friend, in preaching a centenary sermon on the Revolution, November 5, 1788, denounced the essay as heretical, and the author as one who "with one hand receivèd the privileges of the church, while with the other he was endeavoring to plunge the keenest poniard into her heart." M'Gill published a defence, which led, in April, 1789, to the introduction of the case into the presbyterial court of Ayr, and subsequently into that of the synod of Glasgow and Ayr. Meanwhile, the public out of doors was agitating the question with the keenest interest, and the strife of the liberal and zealous parties in the church had reached a painful extreme. It was now that Burns took up the pen in behalf of M'Gill, whom he looked on as a worthy and enlightened person suffering an unworthy persecution.

Orthodox, orthodox,
Wha believe in John Knox,
Let me sound an alarm to your conscience;
There's a heretic blast
Has been blawn in the wast,
That what is not sense must be nonsense.

Dr. Mac, Dr. Mac,
You should stretch on a rack,
To strike evildoers wi' terror;

To join faith and sense,
Upon any pretence,
Is heretic, damnable error.

Town of Ayr, town of Ayr,[1]
It was mad, I declare,
To meddle wi' mischief a-brewing;
Provost John [2] is still deaf
To the church's relief,
And Orator Bob [3] is its ruin.

D'rmple mild,[4] D'rymple mild,
Though your heart's like a child,
And your life like the new-driven snaw;
Yet that winna save ye,

1 When Dr. M'Gill's case first came before the synod, the magistrates of Ayr published an advertisement in the newspapers, bearing a warm testimony to the excellence of the defender's character, and their appreciation of his services as a pastor.

2 John Ballantyne, Esq., banker, provost of Ayr, the prime mover, probably, in the testimony in favor of Dr. M'Gill — the same individual to whom *The Twa Brigs* is dedicated. There could not have been a nobler instance of true benevolence and manly worth than that furnished by Provost Ballantyne. His hospitable mansion was known far and wide, and he was the friend of every liberal measure.

3 Mr. Robert Aiken, writer in Ayr, to whom the *Cotter's Saturday Night* is inscribed. He exerted his powerful oratorical talents as agent for M'Gill in the presbytery and synod.

4 The Rev. Dr. William Dalrymple, senior minister of the collegiate charge of Ayr — a man of extraordinary benevolence and worth. If we are to believe the poet, his views respecting the Trinity had not been strictly orthodox.

Auld Satan must have ye,
For preaching that three's ane and twa.

Rumble John,[1] Rumble John,
Mount the steps wi' a groan,
Cry, the book is wi' heresy crammed;
Then lug out your ladle,
Deal brimstone like adle, muck-water
And roar every note of the damned.

Simper James,[2] Simper James,
Leave the fair Killie dames,
There's a holier chase in your view;
I'll lay on your head,
That the pack ye'll soon lead,
For puppies like you there's but few.

Singet Sawney,[3] Singet Sawney,
Are ye huirding the penny, hoarding
Unconscious what evils await;
Wi' a jump, yell, and howl,
Alarm every soul,
For the foul thief is just at your gate.

Daddy Auld,[4] Daddy Auld,
There's a tod in the fauld, fox

1 The Rev. John Russell, celebrated in *The Holy Fair.*

2 The Rev. James Mackinlay, minister of Kilmarnock, the hero of *The Ordination.*

3 The Rev. Mr. Alexander Moodie, of Riccarton, one of the heroes of *The Twa Herds.*

4 The Rev. Mr. Auld, of Mauchline.

A tod meikle waur than the clerk;[1]
Though ye downa do skaith, cannot — harm
Ye'll be in at the death,
And if ye canna bite, ye may bark.

Davie Bluster,[2] Davie Bluster,
For a saint if ye muster,
The corps is no nice of recruits;
Yet to worth let's be just,
Royal blood ye might boast,
If the ass was the king of the brutes.

Jamy Goose,[3] Jamy Goose,
Ye hae made but toom roose, empty praise
In hunting the wicked lieutenant;
But the Doctor's your mark,
For the L—d's haly ark,
He has cooper'd and cawt a wrong pin in't. driven

Poet Willie,[4] Poet Willie,
Gie the Doctor a volley,

1 The clerk was Mr. Gavin Hamilton, whose defence against the charges preferred by Mr. Auld, as elsewhere stated, had occasioned much trouble to this clergyman.

2 Mr. Grant, Ochiltree.

3 Mr. Young, Cumnock.

4 The Rev. Dr. Peebles. He had excited some ridicule by a line in a poem on the Centenary of the Revolution:

"And bound in *Liberty's* endearing *chain.*"

The poetry of this gentleman is said to have been indifferent. He attempted wit in private conversation with no better success.

Wi' your "Liberty's chain" and your wit;
O'er Pegasus' side
Ye ne'er laid a stride,
Ye but smelt, man, the place where he ——.

Andro Gouk,[1] Andro Gouk,
Ye may slander the book,
And the book not the waur, let me tell ye;
Ye are rich, and look big,
But lay by hat and wig,
And ye'll hae a calf's head o' sma' value.

Barr Steenie,[2] Barr Steenie,
What mean ye — what mean ye?
If ye'll meddle nae mair wi' the matter,
Ye may hae some pretence
To havins and sense, manners
Wi' people wha ken ye nae better.

Irvine-side,[3] Irvine-side,
Wi' your turkey-cock pride,

[1] Dr. Andrew Mitchell, Monkton. Extreme love of money, and a strange confusion of ideas, characterized this presbyter. In his prayer for the royal family, he would express himself thus: "Bless the King — his Majesty the Queen — her Majesty the Prince of Wales."

[2] Rev. Stephen Young, Barr.

[3] Rev. George Smith, Galston. This gentleman is praised as friendly to Common Sense in *The Holy Fair*. The offence which was taken at that praise probably imbittered the poet against him.

Of manhood but sma' is your share;
    Ye've the figure, 'tis true,
    Even your faes will allow,
And your friends they dare grant you nae mair.

    Muirland Jock,[1] Muirland Jock,
    Whom the L—d made a rock
To crush Common Sense for her sins,
    If ill manners were wit,
    There's no mortal so fit
To confound the poor Doctor at ance.

    Holy Will,[2] Holy Will,
    There was wit i' your skull,
When ye pilfered the alms o' the poor;
    The timmer is scant, timber
    When ye're ta'en for a saunt,
Wha should swing in a rape for a hour. rope

    Calvin's sons, Calvin's sons,
    Seize your spir'tual guns,
Ammunition you never can need;
    Your hearts are the stuff,

1 Rev. John Shepherd, Muirkirk. The statistical account of Muirkirk, contributed by this gentleman to Sir John Sinclair's work, is above the average in intelligence, and very agreeably written. He had, however, an unfortunate habit of saying rude things, which he mistook for wit, and thus laid himself open to Burns's satire.

2 The elder, William Fisher, whom Burns had formerly scourged.

Will be powther enough,
And your skulls are storehouses o' lead.

Poet Burns, Poet Burns,
Wi' your priest-skelping turns, slapping
Why desert ye your auld native shire?
Though your Muse is a gipsy,
Yet were she e'en tipsy,
She could ca' us nae waur than we are.[1]

[1] In the present version of this poem, advantage is taken of a few various readings from a copy published by Allan Cunningham, in which there is a curious repetition of the last line of each verse, along with the name of the party addressed. A specimen of this arrangement is given in the following additional stanza, from Allan's copy: —

Afton's laird, Afton's laird,
When your pen can be spared,
A copy of this I bequeath
On the same sicker score,
As I mentioned before,
To that trusty auld worthy, Clackleith,
Afton's laird;
To that trusty auld worthy, Clackleith.

WILLIE BREWED A PECK O' MAUT.

"This air is [Allan] Masterton's; the song, mine. The occasion of it was this: Mr. William Nicol, of the High School, Edinburgh, during the autumn vacation being at Moffat, honest Allan — who was at that time on a visit to Dalswinton — and I went to pay Nicol a visit. We had such a joyous meeting, that Mr. Masterton and I agreed, each in our own way, that we should celebrate the business." — *B.*

O Willie brewed a peck o' maut,
  And Rob and Allan cam to pree: taste
Three blither hearts that lee-lang night
  Ye wad na find in Christendie.
    We are na fou', we're nae that fou',
      But just a drappie in our e'e;
    The cock may craw, the day may daw,
      And aye we'll taste the barley-bree.

Here are we met, three merry boys,
  Three merry boys, I trow, are we;
And monie a night we've merry been,
  And monie mae we hope to be!

It is the moon, I ken her horn,
  That's blinkin' in the lift sae hie; sky

She shines sae bright to wile us hame,
But, by my sooth, she'll wait a wee!

Wha first shall rise to gang awa',
A cuckold, coward loon is he!
Wha last beside his chair shall fa',[1]
He is the king amang us three!

THE WHISTLE.

"In the train of Anne of Denmark, when she came to Scotland with our James VI., there came over also a Danish gentleman of gigantic stature and great prowess, and a matchless champion of Bacchus. He had a little ebony whistle, which at the commencement of the orgies he laid on the table, and whoever was the last able to blow it, everybody else being disabled by the potency of the bottle, was to carry off the whistle as a trophy of victory. The Dane produced credentials of his victories, without a single defeat, at the courts of Copenhagen, Stockholm, Moscow, Warsaw, and several of the petty courts in Germany; and challenged the Scots Bacchanalians to the alternative of trying his prowess, or else of acknowledging their inferiority. After many overthrows on the part of the

[1] In Johnson's *Museum* —

"Wha first beside his chair shall fa'."

Evidently a mistake.

Scots, the Dane was encountered by Sir Robert Lawrie of Maxwelton, ancestor of the present worthy baronet of that name; who, after three days and three nights' hard contest, left the Scandinavian under the table,

'And blew on the whistle his requiem shrill.'

Sir Walter, son to Sir Robert before mentioned, afterwards lost the whistle to Walter Riddel of Glenriddel, who had married a sister of Sir Walter's." [1] — *B.*

The whistle being now in the possession of Captain Riddel, Burns's neighbor at Friars' Carse, it was resolved that he should submit it to an amicable contest, involving, besides himself, two other descendants of the conqueror of the Scandinavian — namely, Mr. Fergusson of Craigdarroch, and Sir Robert Lawrie of Maxwelton, then M. P. for Dumfriesshire. The meeting was to take place at Friars' Carse on Friday the 16th of October.

A note was sent to Burns, inviting him to join the party at Carse. He immediately replied in characteristic fashion.

The king's poor blackguard slave am I,
And scarce dow spare a minute; can
But I'll be with you by and bye,
Or else the devil's in it!

R. B.

[1] Mr. C. K. Sharpe has shown from a pedigree of the Maxwelton family that the story of the toping Dane "may be regarded as a groundless fable, unless such a person came over in the train of Prince George of Denmark, the husband of our last Queen Anne, which is not very probable." — *2d edition of Johnson's Musical Museum* (1839) iv. 362.

He was, accordingly, present, if not at the dinner, at the compotation which followed; and the whole affair has been by him chronicled in the most glowing phraseology in his poem.

I SING of a whistle, a whistle of worth,
I sing of a whistle, the pride of the North,
Was brought to the court of our good Scottish
 king,
And long with this whistle all Scotland shall
 ring.

Old Loda,[1] still rueing the arm of Fingal,
The god of the bottle sends down from his
 hall:
"This whistle's your challenge — to Scotland
 get o'er,
And drink them to hell, sir! or ne'er see me
 more!"

Old poets have sung, and old chronicles tell,
What champions ventured, what champions fell;
The son of great Loda was conqueror still,
And blew on the whistle his requiem shrill;

Till Robert, the lord of the Cairn and the
 Skarr,[2]
Unmatched at the bottle, unconquered in war,

[1] See Ossian's Caric-thura. — *B.*

[2] The Cairn, a stream in Glencairn parish, on which Max-

He drank his poor godship as deep as the sea—
No tide of the Baltic e'er drunker than he.

Thus Robert, victorious, the trophy has gained,
Which now in his house has for ages remained;
Till three noble chieftains, and all of his blood,
The jovial contest again have renewed.

Three joyous good fellows, with hearts clear of flaw:
Craigdarroch, so famous for wit, worth, and law;
And trusty Glenriddel, so skilled in old coins;
And gallant Sir Robert, deep-read in old wines.

Craigdarroch began, with a tongue smooth as oil,
Desiring Glenriddel to yield up the spoil;
Or else he would muster the heads of the clan,
And once more, in claret, try which was the man.

"By the gods of the ancients!" Glenriddel replies,
"Before I surrender so glorious a prize,
I'll conjure the ghost of the great Rorie More,[1]
And bumper his horn with him twenty times o'er."

welton House is situated; the Skarr, a similar mountain-rill, in the parish of Penpont; both being affluents of the Nith.

[1] See Johnson's *Tour to the Hebrides.*—*B.*

Sir Robert, a soldier, no speech would pretend,
But he ne'er turned his back on his foe — or his friend ;
Said, Toss down the whistle, the prize of the field,
And knee-deep in claret, he'd die, or he'd yield.

To the board of Glenriddel our heroes repair,
So noted for drowning of sorrow and care;
But for wine and for welcome not more known to fame
Than the sense, wit, and taste of a sweet lovely dame.

A bard was selected to witness the fray,
And tell future ages the feats of the day;
A bard who detested all sadness and spleen,
And wished that Parnassus a vineyard had been.

The dinner being over, the claret they ply,
And every new cork is a new spring of joy;
In the bands of old friendship and kindred so set,
And the bands grew the tighter the more they were wet.

Gay Pleasure ran riot as bumpers ran o'er;
Bright Phœbus ne'er witnessed so joyous a core,

And vowed that to leave them he was quite forlorn,
Till Cynthia hinted he'd see them next morn.

Six bottles apiece had well wore out the night,
When gallant Sir Robert, to finish the fight,
Turned o'er in one bumper a bottle of red,
And swore 'twas the way that their ancestor did.

Then worthy Glenriddel, so cautious and sage,
No longer the warfare, ungodly, would wage;
A high ruling-elder to wallow in wine![1]
He left the foul business to folks less divine.

The gallant Sir Robert fought hard to the end;
But who can with fate and quart-bumpers contend?
Though fate said—a hero shall perish in light;
So up rose bright Phœbus—and down fell the knight.

Next up rose our bard, like a prophet in drink:
"Craigdarroch, thou'lt soar when creation shall sink;

[1] The elder of the Scottish church is called a ruling-elder when sent to represent a burgh in the General Assembly. Glenriddel represented the burgh of Dumfries in several successive assemblies.

But if thou would flourish immortal in rhyme,
Come — one bottle more — and have at the sublime!

"Thy line, that have struggled for freedom with Bruce,
Shall heroes and patriots ever produce:
So thine be the laurel, and mine be the bay;
The field thou hast won, by yon bright god of day!"[1]

TO MARY IN HEAVEN.

The grave had closed over Mary Campbell, as far as our facts and arguments will allow us to assign a date, in the latter part of October, 1786. A day came at the end of harvest, in 1789,[2] when the death of Mary three years before was recalled to the poet. According to Mr. Lockhart, reporting the statement of Mrs. Burns to her friend Mr. M'Diarmid, Burns "spent that day, though laboring under cold, in the usual work of

[1] The whistle remained in the possession of the late Mr. R. C. Fergusson of Craigdarroch, M.P. for the Stewartry of Kirkcudbright, son of the victor.

[2] Mr. Lockhart assigns this incident to September, Chambers to October. The arguments for the latter date are given in the Appendix to Chambers's third volume.

the harvest, and apparently in excellent spirits. But as the twilight deepened, he appeared to grow 'very sad about something,' and at length wandered out into the barn-yard, to which his wife, in her anxiety, followed him, entreating him in vain to observe that frost had set in, and to return to the fireside. On being again and again requested to do so, he promised compliance; but still remained where he was, striding up and down slowly, and contemplating the sky, which was singularly clear and starry. At last Mrs. Burns found him stretched on a mass of straw, with his eyes fixed on a beautiful planet 'that shone like another moon,' and prevailed on him to come in. He immediately, on entering the house, called for his desk, and wrote exactly as they now stand, with all the ease of one copying from memory, these sublime and pathetic verses."

THOU ling'ring star, with less'ning ray,
  That lov'st to greet the early morn,
Again thou usher'st in the day
  My Mary from my soul was torn.
O Mary! dear departed shade!
  Where is thy place of blissful rest?
See'st thou thy lover lowly laid?
  Hear'st thou the groans that rend his breast?

That sacred hour can I forget,
  Can I forget the hallowed grove,
Where by the winding Ayr we met,
  To live one day of parting love!

Eternity will not efface
  Those records dear of transports past,
Thy image at our last embrace, —
  Ah! little thought we 'twas our last!

Ayr, gurgling, kissed his pebbled shore,
  O'erhung with wild woods, thick'ning green;
The fragrant birch, and hawthorn hoar,
  Twined am'rous round the raptured scene;
The flowers sprang wanton to be prest,
  The birds sang love on every spray —
Till too, too soon, the glowing west
  Proclaimed the speed of wingèd day.

Still o'er these scenes my mem'ry wakes,
  And fondly broods with miser care;
Time but th' impression stronger makes,
  As streams their channels deeper wear.
My Mary! dear departed shade!
  Where is thy place of blissful rest?
See'st thou thy lover lowly laid?
  Hear'st thou the groans that rend his breast?

TO DR. BLACKLOCK.

Burns had written a letter about the late changes in his circumstances to his venerable friend Blacklock, and intrusted it to Robert Heron, a young scion of the church connected with the south-western district of Scotland, and who was now beginning to busy himself with literary speculations. Heron had proved a faithless messenger, and Blacklock had addressed Burns a rhyming letter of kind inquiries; to which Burns replied as follows.

ELLISLAND, 21*st Oct.*, 1789.

Wow, but your letter made me vauntie! elated
And are ye hale, and weel, and cantie? merry
I kenned it still your wee bit jauntie,
Wad bring ye to:
Lord send you aye as weel's I want ye,
And then ye'll do.

The ill-thief blaw the Heron south! devil
And never drink be near his drouth!
He tauld mysel' by word o' mouth,
He'd tak my letter;
I lippened to the chield in trouth, trusted
And bade nae better. desired

But aiblins honest Master Heron — perhaps
Had at the time some dainty fair one,
To ware his theologic care on, — spend
And holy study;
And tired o' sauls to waste his lear on, — learning
E'en tried the body.

But what d'ye think, my trusty fier? — comrade
I'm turned a gauger — Peace be here!
Parnassian queans, I fear, I fear,
Ye'll now disdain me!
And then my fifty pounds a year
Will little gain me.

Ye glaikèt, gleesome, dainty damies, — giddy
Wha, by Castalia's wimplin' streamies, — winding
Lowp, sing, and lave your pretty limbies, — leap
Ye ken, ye ken,
That strang Necessity supreme is
'Mang sons o' men.

I hae a wife and twa wee laddies,
They maun hae brose and brats o' duddies; — pottage — suits of clothes
Ye ken yoursels my heart right proud is —
I need na vaunt,
But I'll sned besoms — thraw saugh woodies,[1]
Before they want.

[1] Cut birches for brooms, and twist willow twigs to bind them. Woodies — "two or three willow twigs twisted to-

Lord, help me through this warld o' care!
I'm weary sick o't late and air! early
Not but I hae a richer share
Than monie ithers;
But why should ae man better fare,
And a' men brithers?

Come, firm Resolve, take thou the van,
Thou stalk o' carl-hemp[1] in man!
And let us mind, faint heart ne'er wan
A lady fair:
Wha does the utmost that he can,
Will whyles do mair. sometimes

But to conclude my silly rhyme
(I'm scant o' verse, and scant o' time),
To make a happy fireside clime
To weans and wife, little ones
That's the true pathos and sublime
Of human life.

My compliments to Sister Beckie,
And eke the same to honest Lucky;
I wat she is a dainty chuckie,[2]

gether, used for binding the end of a broom or birch besom." — *Dr. Jamieson.*

1 The male hemp, that which bears the seed; "Ye have a stalk o' carl-hemp in you," is a Scotch proverb. — *Kelly.*

2 Chuckie, a familiar term for a hen, transferred endearingly to a matron of the human species.

As e'er tread clay!
And gratefully, my guid auld cockie,
I'm yours for aye.
ROBERT BURNS.

ON CAPTAIN GROSE'S PEREGRINATIONS THROUGH SCOTLAND,

COLLECTING THE ANTIQUITIES OF THAT KINGDOM.

Francis Grose was a broken-down English gentleman who, under the impulse of poverty, had been induced to exercise considerable literary and artistic talents for the benefit of the public. A large work on the Antiquities of England had been completed some years ago. He had also produced a treatise on Arms and Armour, another on Military Antiquities, and several minor works. The genius and social spirit of the man were scarcely more remarkable than his personal figure, which was ludicrously squat and obese. Grose having made an inroad into Scotland, for the purpose of sketching and chronicling its antiquities, Burns met him at Friars' Carse, and was greatly amused by his aspect and conversation. The comic Muse also caught at the antiquarian enthusiasm as a proper subject.

HEAR, Land o' Cakes, and brither Scots,
Frae Maidenkirk [1] to Johnny Groat's;

[1] Maidenkirk is an inversion of the name of Kirkmaiden, in Wigtonshire, the most southerly parish in Scotland.

If there's a hole in a' your coats,
I rede you tent it: advise — give heed to
A chiel's amang you taking notes,
And, faith, he'll prent it.

If in your bounds ye chance to light
Upon a fine, fat, fodgel wight, plump
O' stature short, but genius bright,
That's he, mark weel —
And wow! he has an unco slight knack
O' cauk and keel.[1]

By some auld houlet-haunted biggin, owl — building
Or kirk deserted by its riggin', roof
It's ten to ane ye'll find him snug in
Some eldritch part, elfish
Wi' deils, they say, Lord save's! colleaguin'
At some black art.

Ilk ghaist that haunts auld ha' or chaumer, chamber
Ye gipsy-gang that deal in glamour, necromancy
And you deep-read in hell's black grammar,
Warlocks and witches!
Ye'll quake at his conjuring hammer,
Ye midnight bitches.

It's tauld he was a sodger bred,
And ane wad rather fa'n than fled; fallen
But now he's quat the spurtle blade,[2]

[1] Chalk and red or black lead-pencil.

[2] A spurtle is a stick with which pottage, gruel, etc., are stirred when boiling; used here like "toasting-iron."

And dog-skin wallet,
And ta'en the — Antiquarian trade,
I think they call it.

He has a fouth o' auld nick-nackets, abundance
Rusty airn caps and jinglin' jackets,
Wad haud the Lothians three in keep
tackets, shoe-nails
A towmont guid; twelvemonth
And parritch-pats, and auld saut-backets,
Before the Flood.

Of Eve's first fire he has a cinder;
Auld Tubalcain's fire-shool and fender; shovel
That which distinguishèd the gender
O' Balaam's ass;
A broomstick o' the witch of Endor,
Weel shod wi' brass.

Forbye, he'll shape you aff, fu' gleg, Besides — quickly
The cut of Adam's philabeg;
The knife that nicket Abel's craig, neck
He'll prove you fully,
It was a faulding jocteleg,[1]
Or lang-kail gully.[2]

[1] "Jocktaleg, a clasp-knife; Northumberland and Scotland. Probably from Jock of Liege. Liege formerly supplied Scotland with cutlery." — *Grose's Provincial Glossary.* "The etymology of this word remained unknown till not many years ago, that an old knife was found, having this inscription *Jacques de Liege*, the name of the cutler. Thus it is in exact analogy with *Andrea di Ferrara.*" — *Lord Hailes.*

[2] A long knife for cutting coleworts.

But wad ye see him in his glee,
(For meikle glee and fun has he,)
Then set him down, and twa or three
Guid fellows wi' him;
And port, O port! shine thou a wee,
And then ye'll see him!

Now, by the powers o' verse and prose!
Thou art a dainty chiel, O Grose!—
Whae'er o' thee shall ill suppose,
They sair misca' thee;
I'd take the rascal by the nose,
Wad say, Shame fa' thee.

EPITAPH ON CAPTAIN GROSE, THE CELEBRATED ANTIQUARY.

The Devil got notice that Grose was a-dying,
So whip! at the summons, old Satan came flying;
But when he approached where poor Francis lay moaning,
And saw each bedpost with its burden a-groaning,
Astonished, confounded, cried Satan: "By ——,
I'll want 'im, ere I take such a damnable load."

WRITTEN IN AN ENVELOPE, ENCLOSING A LETTER TO CAPTAIN GROSE.

Professor Stewart having intimated to the poet a desire to see Grose, Burns sent a letter, notifying Stewart's wish, to his antiquarian friend.

Not being very sure of the whereabouts of Grose, the bard enclosed his letter in an envelope addressed to Mr. Cardonnel, a brother antiquary, and containing a set of jocular verses in imitation of the quaint song of Sir John Malcolm.

Ken ye ought o' Captain Grose?
Igo and ago,
If he's amang his friends or foes?
Iram, coram, dago.

Is he to Abra'm's bosom gane?
Igo and ago;
Or hauding Sarah by the wame?
Iram, coram, dago.

Is he south, or is he north?
Igo and ago;
Or drownèd in the river Forth?
Iram, coram, dago.

Is he slain by Highlan' bodies?
Igo and ago,
And eaten like a wether haggis?
Iram, coram, dago.

Where'er he be, the Lord be near him,
Igo and ago;
As for the deil, he daurna steer him, disturb
Iram, coram, dago.

But please transmit the enclosèd letter,
Igo and ago,
Which will oblige your humble debtor,
Iram, coram, dago.

So may ye hae auld stanes in store,
Igo and ago,
The very stanes that Adam bore,
Iram, coram, dago.

So may ye get in glad possession,
Igo and ago,
The coins o' Satan's coronation!
Iram, coram, dago.

THE LADDIES BY THE BANKS O' NITH.

TUNE — *Up and waur them a'.*

A contest for the representation of the Dumfries group of burghs commenced in September between Sir James Johnston of Westerhall, the previous member, and Captain Miller, younger of Dalswinton, son of Burns's landlord. In this affair the bard stood variously affected. Professing only a whimsical Jacobitism, he had hitherto taken no decided part with either of the two great factions of his time; but he had a certain leaning towards Mr. Pitt and his supporters. On the other hand, some of his best friends— as Henry Erskine, the Earl of Glencairn, Mr. Miller, Captain Riddel — were Whigs, and these persons he was fearful to offend. On this canvass becoming keen, Burns threw in his pen, but rather from the contagion of local excitement than from partisanship. One feeling, indeed, he had in earnest, and this was detestation of the Duke of Queensberry. The duke, who was the greatest landlord in Nithsdale, was considered as having proved something like a traitor to the king on the late occasion of the Regency Bill, when he was in the minority which voted for the surrender of the power of the crown into the hands of the Prince of Wales without restriction. For this, and for his mean personal character and heartless debaucheries, Burns held his Grace in extreme contempt. In the first place, then, he penned an election ballad, chiefly against the duke.

THE laddies by the banks o' Nith
Wad trust his Grace wi' a', Jamie,
But he'll sair them as he sair'd the king — serve
Turn tail and rin awa', Jamie.

Up and waur them a', Jamie, baffle
Up and waur them a';
The Johnstons hae the guidin' o't,[1]
Ye turn-coat Whigs, awa'!

The day he stude his country's friend,
Or gied her faes a claw, Jamie,
Or frae puir man a blessin' wan,
That day the Duke ne'er saw, Jamie.

But wha is he, his country's boast?
Like him there is na twa, Jamie;
There's no a callant tents the kye, boy watches
But kens o' Westerha', Jamie.

[1] A Border proverb, significant of the great local power of this family in former times. The Gordons were the subject of a similar proverb, which forms the title of a beautiful melody.

To end the wark, here's Whistlebirck,[1]
Lang may his whistle blaw, Jamie;
And Maxwell true o' sterling blue,
And we'll be Johnstons a', Jamie.

THE FIVE CARLINES.

In this second election ballad the five burghs are presented under figurative characters most felicitously drawn: Dumfries, as Maggy on the banks of Nith; Annan, as Blinking Bess of Annandale; Kirkcudbright, as Whisky Jean of Galloway; Sanquhar, as Black Joan frae Crichton Peel; and Lochmaben, as Marjory of the many Lochs — appellations all of which have some appropriateness from local circumstances.

THERE were five carlines in the south, old women
They fell upon a scheme,
To send a lad to Lon'on town,
To bring them tidings hame.

Nor only bring them tidings hame,
But do their errands there,

1 Alexander Birtwhistle, Esq., merchant at Kirkcudbright, and provost of the burgh.

And aiblins gowd and honour baith possibly
  Might be that laddie's share.

There was Maggy by the banks o' Nith,
  A dame wi' pride eneugh,
And Marjory o' the Monie Lochs,
  A carline auld and teugh.

And Blinking Bess o' Annandale,
  That dwelt near Solwayside,
And Whisky Jean, that took her gill,
  In Galloway sae wide.

And Black Joan, frae Crichton Peel,
  O' gipsy kith and kin —
Five wighter carlines warna foun' brisker, stouter
  The south countra within.

To send a lad to Lon'on town,
  They met upon a day,
And monie a knight and monie a laird
  Their errand fain would gae.

O monie a knight and monie a laird
  This errand fain would gae;
But nae ane could their fancy please,
  O ne'er a ane but twae.

The first he was a belted knight,[1]
  Bred o' a Border clan,

[1] Sir James Johnston.

And he wad gae to Lon'on town,
 Might nae man him withstan'.

And he wad do their errands weel,
 And meikle he wad say,
And ilka ane at Lon'on court
 Would bid to him guid-day.

Then next came in a sodger youth,[1]
 And spak wi' modest grace,
And he wad gae to Lon'on town,
 If sae their pleasure was.

He wadna hecht them courtly gifts, promise
 Nor meikle speech pretend,
But he wad hecht an honest heart
 Wad ne'er desert a friend.

Now, wham to choose, and wham refuse,
 At strife thir carlines fell; these
For some had gentle folks to please,
 And some wad please themsel'.

Then out spak mim-mou'ed Meg o' Nith, prim-mouthed
 And she spak up wi' pride,
And she wad send the sodger youth,
 Whatever might betide.

[1] Captain Miller.

For the auld guidman o' Lon'on court[1]
  She didna care a pin;
But she wad send the sodger youth
  To greet his eldest son.[2]

Then up sprang Bess o' Annandale,
  And a deadly aith she's ta'en,
That she wad vote the Border knight,
  Though she should vote her lane. alone

For far-aff fowls hae feathers fair,
  And fools o' change are fain;
But I hae tried the Border knight,
  And I'll try him yet again.

Says Black Joan frae Crichton Peel,
  A carline stoor and grim, austere
"The auld guidman, and the young guidman,
  For me may sink or swim.

"For fools will freit[3] o' right or wrang,
  While knaves laugh them to scorn;
But the sodger's friends hae blawn the best,
  So he shall bear the horn."

Then Whisky Jean spak owre her drink,
  "Ye weel ken, kimmers a', gossips

1 The King.
2 The Prince of Wales.
3 Talk superstitiously.

The auld guidman o' Lon'on court
  His back's been at the wa';

"And monie a friend that kissed his cup
  Is now a fremit wight: estranged
But it's ne'er be said o' Whisky Jean —
  I'll send the Border knight."

Then slow raise Marjory o' the Lochs,
  And wrinkled was her brow,
Her ancient weed was russet gray,
  Her auld Scots bluid was true; [1]

"There's some great folks set light by me —
  I set as light by them;
But I will send to Lon'on town
  Wham I like best at hame.

"Sae how this weighty plea may end
  Nae mortal wight can tell:
God grant the king and ilka man
  May look weel to himsel'."

[1] It may not be unworthy of notice that this verse was one in great favor with Sir Walter Scott, who used to recite it with good effect.

THE BLUE-EYED LASSIE.[1]

Mr. Jeffrey, the clergyman of Lochmaben, had a daughter, a sweet blue-eyed young creature, who at one of Burns's visits, did the honors of the table. Next morning, our poet presented at breakfast a song which has given the young lady immortality.

I GAED a waefu' gate yestreen, road
A gate, I fear, I'll dearly rue;
I gat my death frae twa sweet een,
Twa lovely een o' bonny blue.
'Twas not her golden ringlets bright,
Her lips like roses wat wi' dew,
Her heaving bosom, lily-white —
It was her een sae bonny blue.

She talked, she smiled, my heart she wiled;
She charmed my soul — I wist na how;
And aye the stound, the deadly wound, pang
Cam fra her een sae bonny blue.

[1] This song was printed in Johnson's *Museum*, with an air composed by Mr. Riddel of Glenriddel. It has been set by George Thomson to the tune of "*The Blathrie o't*," but, in the opinion of the present editor, it flows much more sweetly to "*My only joe and dearie O.*"

But, spare to speak, and spare to speed;[1]
  She'll aiblins listen to my vow; perhaps
Should she refuse, I'll lay my dead death
  To her twa een sae bonny blue.

SONG.

AIR — *Maggy Lauder.*

Miss Jeffrey married a gentleman named Renwick, of New York, and was living there about 1822, when a son of Mr. George Thomson was introduced to her by her son, the professor of chemistry in Columbia College.

The following song has been put forward as another composition of Burns in honor of the "Blue-eyed Lassie." It first appeared in the *New York Mirror* (1846).

WHEN first I saw fair Jeanie's face,
  I couldna tell what ailed me,
My heart went fluttering pit-a-pat,
  My een they almost failed me.
She's aye sae neat, sae trim, sae tight,
  All grace does round her hover,
Ae look deprived me o' my heart,
  And I became a lover.

[1] A proverbial expression.

She's aye, aye sae blithe, sae gay,
  She's aye so blithe and cheerie;
She's aye sae bonny, blithe, and gay,
  O gin I were her dearie!

Had I Dundas's whole estate,
  Or Hopetoun's wealth to shine in;
Did warlike laurels crown my brow,
  Or humbler bays entwining;
I'd lay them a' at Jeanie's feet,
  Could I but hope to move her,
And prouder than a belted knight,
  I'd be my Jeanie's lover.
    She's aye, aye sae blithe, sae gay, etc.

But sair I fear some happier swain
  Has gained sweet Jeanie's favour:
If so, may every bliss be hers,
  Though I maun never have her,
But gang she east, or gang she west,
  'Twixt Forth and Tweed all over,
While men have eyes, or ears, or taste,
  She'll always find a lover.
    She's aye, aye sae blithe, sae gay, etc.

SKETCH — NEW-YEAR'S DAY [1790].

TO MRS. DUNLOP.

This day, Time winds the exhausted chain,
To run the twelvemonth's length again:
I see the old, bald-pated fellow,
With ardent eyes, complexion sallow,
Adjust the unimpaired machine,
To wheel the equal, dull routine.

The absent lover, minor heir,
In vain assail him with their prayer;
Deaf as my friend, he sees them press,
Nor makes the hour one moment less.
Will you (the Major's[1] with the hounds;
The happy tenants share his rounds;
Coila's fair Rachel's[2] care to-day,
And blooming Keith's engaged with Gray)
From housewife cares a minute borrow —
That grandchild's cap will do to-morrow —

1 Afterwards General Dunlop of Dunlop.

2 Rachel, a daughter of Mrs. Dunlop, was making a sketch of Coila.

And join with me a moralising,
This day's propitious to be wise in.
First, what did yesternight deliver?
"Another year is gone for ever."

And what is this day's strong suggestion?
"The passing moment's all we rest on!"
Rest on — for what? what do we here?
Or why regard the passing year?
Will Time, amused with proverbed lore,
Add to our date one minute more?
A few days may — a few years must —
Repose us in the silent dust.
Then is it wise to damp our bliss?
Yes — all such reasonings are amiss!
The voice of Nature loudly cries,
And many a message from the skies,
That something in us never dies:
That on this frail, uncertain state,
Hang matters of eternal weight:
That future life in worlds unknown
Must take its hue from this alone;
Whether as heavenly glory bright,
Or dark as Misery's woeful night.
Since, then, my honoured, first of friends,
On this poor being all depends,
Let us the important *now* employ,
And live as those who never die.
Though you, with days and honours crowned
Witness that filial circle round

(A sight Life's sorrows to repulse,
A sight pale Envy to convulse),
Others now claim your chief regard;
Yourself, you wait your bright reward.

PROLOGUE,

SPOKEN AT THE THEATRE, DUMFRIES, ON NEW-YEAR'S DAY EVENING [1790].

"We have got a set of very decent players here just now. I have seen them an evening or two. David Campbell, in Ayr, wrote to me by the manager of the company, a Mr. Sutherland, who is a man of apparent worth. On New-year's Day evening, I gave him the following prologue, which he spouted to his audience with applause." — *Burns to his brother Gilbert, 11th January,* 1790.

No song nor dance I bring from yon great city
That queens it o'er our taste — the more's the
pity:
Though, by the by, abroad why will you roam?
Good sense and taste are natives here at home.
But not for panegyric I appear,
I come to wish you all a good New Year!
Old Father Time deputes me here before ye,
Not for to preach, but tell his simple story:

The sage grave ancient coughed, and bade me say:
"You're one year older this important day."
If wiser, too — he hinted some suggestion,
But 'twould be rude, you know, to ask the question;
And with a would-be roguish leer and wink,
He bade me on you press this one word — "think!"

Ye sprightly youths, quite flushed with hope and spirit,
Who think to storm the world by dint of merit,
To you the dotard has a deal to say,
In his sly, dry, sententious, proverb way.
He bids you mind, amid your thoughtless rattle,
That the first blow is ever half the battle;
That though some by the skirt may try to snatch him,
Yet by the forelock is the hold to catch him;
That whether doing, suffering, or forbearing,
You may do miracles by persevering.
Last, though not least in love, ye youthful fair,
Angelic forms, high Heaven's peculiar care!
To you old Bald-pate smooths his wrinkled brow,
And humbly begs you'll mind the important Now!
To crown your happiness he asks your leave,
And offers bliss to give and to receive.

For our sincere, though haply weak endeavours,
With grateful pride we own your many favours;
And howsoe'er our tongues may ill reveal it,
Believe our glowing bosoms truly feel it.

MY LOVELY NANCY.

TUNE — *The Quaker's Wife.*

About this time [the end of January, 1790,] the Clarinda correspondence was for a moment renewed. Burns closed his first letter with the following song, being, he says, one of his latest productions. From few men besides Burns could any lady have expected, along with an apology for deserting her only twenty months ago, a pleasant-faced canzonet of compliment declaring the world to be lightless without love.

THINE am I, my faithful fair,
Thine, my lovely Nancy;
Every pulse along my veins,
Every roving fancy.

To thy bosom lay my heart,
There to throb and languish:

Though despair had wrung its core,
  That would heal its anguish.

Take away those rosy lips,
  Rich with balmy treasure;
Turn away thine eyes of love,
  Lest I die with pleasure.

What is life when wanting love?
  Night without a morning:
Love's the cloudless summer sun,
  Nature gay adorning.

PROLOGUE FOR MR. SUTHERLAND'S BENEFIT-NIGHT, DUMFRIES.

Towards the conclusion of the theatrical season at Dumfries, Coila came once more to the aid of Mr. Manager Sutherland; but it cannot be said that her effusion was such as to hold forth a very favorable prognostic of dramatic effort.

WHAT needs this din about the town o' Lon'on,
How this new play and that new sang is comin'?
Why is outlandish stuff sae meikle courted?
Does nonsense mend, like whisky, when imported?

Is there nae poet, burning keen for fame,
Will try to gie us songs and plays at hame?
For comedy abroad he needna toil;
A fool and knave are plants of every soil.
Nor need he hunt as far as Rome and Greece
To gather matter for a serious piece:
There's themes enough in Caledonian story,
Would shew the tragic Music in a' her glory.

Is there no daring bard will rise, and tell
How glorious Wallace stood, how hapless fell?
Where are the Muses fled that could produce
A drama worthy o' the name o' Bruce?
How here, even here, he first unsheathed the sword
'Gainst mighty England and her guilty lord;
And after monie a bloody, deathless doing,
Wrenched his dear country from the jaws of ruin?
O for a Shakspeare or an Otway scene,
To draw the lovely, hapless Scottish Queen!
Vain all th' omnipotence of female charms
'Gainst headlong, ruthless, mad rebellion's arms.
She fell, but fell with spirit truly Roman,
To glut the vengeance of a rival woman:
A woman — though the phrase may seem uncivil —
As able and as cruel as the devil!
One Douglas lives in Home's immortal page,
But Douglasses were heroes every age:

And though your fathers, prodigal of life,
A Douglas followed to the martial strife,
Perhaps if bowls row right, and Right succeeds, roll
Ye yet may follow where a Douglas leads!
As *ye* hae generous done, if a' the land
Would take the Muses' servants by the hand;
Not only hear, but patronise, befriend them,
And where ye justly can commend, commend them;
And aiblins when they winna stand the test, perhaps
Wink hard, and say the folks hae done their best!
Would a' the land do this, then I'll be caution
Ye'll soon hae poets o' the Scottish nation,
Will gar Fame blaw until her trumpet crack,
And warsle Time, and lay him on his back! strive with
For us and for our stage should ony spier, ask
"Wha's aught thae chiels maks a' this bustle here?" Who are those fellows
My best leg foremost, I'll set up my brow, —
We have the honour to belong to you!
We're your ain bairns, e'en guide us as ye like,
But like guid mithers, shore before you strike. threaten
And gratefu' still I hope ye'll ever find us,
For a' the patronage and meikle kindness
We've got frae a' professions, sets, and ranks:
God help us! we're but poor — ye'se get but thanks.

CONTRIBUTIONS

TO THE THIRD VOLUME OF JOHNSON'S MUSEUM.

TIBBIE DUNBAR.

TUNE—*Johnny M'Gill.*

The third volume of the *Scots Musical Museum* had been going on, somewhat more slowly than the second, but with an equal amount of assistance from Burns. Besides the songs already cited since the date of the second volume, he contributed many which, as they bore no particular reference to his own history, nor any other trait by which the exact date of their composition could be ascertained, are here presented in one group. Several of them are, however, only old songs mended or extended by Burns.

O WILT thou go wi' me, sweet Tibbie Dunbar?
O wilt thou go wi' me, sweet Tibbie Dunbar?
Wilt thou ride on a horse or be drawn in a car,
Or walk by my side, sweet Tibbie Dunbar?

I carena thy daddie, his lands and his money,
I carena thy kin, sae high and sae lordly;
But say thou wilt hae me, for better for waur,
And come in thy coatie, sweet Tibbie Dunbar!

THE GARDENER WI' HIS PAIDLE.

Tune—*The Gardeners' March.*

It will be found that Burns subsequently produced a new version of this song, changing the burden at the close of the stanzas.

When rosy Morn comes in wi' showers,
To deck her gay green birken bowers,
Then busy, busy are his hours,
The gardener wi' his paidle.[1]

The crystal waters gently fa',
The merry birds are lovers a',
The scented breezes round him blaw,
The gardener wi' his paidle.

When purple Morning starts the hare,
To steal upon her early fare,
Then through the dews he maun repair,
The gardener wi' his paidle.

When Day, expiring in the west,
The curtain draws of Nature's rest,
He flies to her arms he lo'es the best,
The gardener wi' his paidle.

[1] A long staff with an iron spike, serving sometimes as a narrow spade.

HIGHLAND HARRY.

Of this song Burns says: "The chorus I picked up from an old woman in Dunblane; the rest of the song is mine." It is evident that the poet has understood the chorus in a Jacobite sense, and written his own verses in that strain accordingly. Mr. Peter Buchan has, nevertheless, ascertained that the original song related to a love attachment between Harry Lumsdale, the second son of a Highland gentleman, and Miss Jeanie Gordon, daughter to the Laird of Knockespock, in Aberdeenshire. The lady was married to her cousin, Habichie Gordon, a son of the Laird of Rhynie; and some time after, her former lover having met her and shaken her hand, her husband drew his sword in anger, and lopped off several of Lumsdale's fingers, which Highland Harry took so much to heart that he soon after died. — See Hogg and Motherwell's edition of Burns, ii. 197.

My Harry was a gallant gay,
  Fu' stately strode he on the plain:
But now he's banished far away;
  I'll never see him back again.
    O for him back again!
      O for him back again!
    I wad gie a' Knockhaspie's land
      For Highland Harry back again.

When a' the lave gae to their bed, rest
I wander dowie up the glen; sad
I set me down and greet my fill, cry
And aye I wish him back again.

O were some villains hangit high,
And ilka body had their ain!
Then I might see the joyfu' sight,
My Highland Harry back again.

BONNY ANN.

Air — *Ye Gallants Bright.*

"I composed this song out of compliment to Miss Ann Masterton, the daughter of my friend Allan Masterton, the author of the air 'Strathallan's Lament,' and two or three others in this work." — *Burns.* Miss Masterton afterwards became Mrs. Derbishire, and was living in London in 1834.

Ye gallants bright, I rede ye right, advise
Beware o' bonny Ann;
Her comely face sae fu' o' grace,
Your heart she will trepan.
Her een sae bright, like stars by night,
Her skin is like the swan;

Sae jimply laced her genty waist, slenderly—slim
That sweetly ye might span.

Youth, Grace, and Love, attendant move,
And Pleasure leads the van;
In a' their charms and conquering arms
They wait on bonny Ann.
The captive bands may chain the hands,
But love enslaves the man;
Ye gallants braw, I rede you a',
Beware o' bonny Ann!

JOHN ANDERSON.

TUNE—*John Anderson my Jo.*

JOHN ANDERSON my jo, John, dear
When we were first acquent,
Your locks were like the raven,
Your bonny brow was brent; smooth
But now your brow is beld, John, bald
Your locks are like the snaw;
But blessings on your frosty pow,
John Anderson my jo.

John Anderson my jo, John,
We clamb the hill thegither,

And monie a canty day, John, pleasant
We've had wi' ane anither:
Now we maun totter down, John,
But hand in hand we'll go,
And sleep thegither at the foot,
John Anderson my jo.

THE BATTLE OF SHERIFF-MUIR.[1]

TUNE — *Cameronian Rant.*

In this instance Burns has concentrated in his own language a more diffuse song on the same subject, which is understood to have been the composition of Mr. Barclay, a Berean minister of some note about the middle of the last century, uncle to the distinguished anatomist of the same name.

"O CAM ye here the fight to shun,
Or herd the sheep wi' me, man?
Or were ye at the Sherra-muir,
And did the battle see, man?"

[1] "This was written about the time our bard made his tour to the Highlands, 1787." — *Currie.* Gilbert Burns entertained a doubt if the song was by his brother; but for this we can see no just grounds.

"I saw the battle, sair and tough,
And reekin' red ran monie a sheugh; channel
My heart, for fear, gaed sough for sough, sigh
To hear the thuds, and see the cluds, knocks
O' clans frae woods, in tartan duds, clothes
Wha glaumed at kingdoms three, man. grasped

"The red-coat lads, wi' black cockades,
To meet them were na slaw, man;
They rushed and pushed, and bluid outgushed,
And monie a bouk did fa', man: corpse
The great Argyle led on his files,
I wat they glanced for twenty miles:
They hacked and hashed, while broadswords clashed,
And through they dashed, and hewed, and smashed,
Till fey men died awa', man. predestined

"But had you seen the philabegs,
And skyrin tartan trews, man, shining
When in the teeth they dared our Whigs,
And covenant true-blues, man;
In lines extended lang and large,
When bayonets opposed the targe,
And thousands hastened to the charge,
Wi' Highland wrath they frae the sheath
Drew blades o' death, till, out o' breath,
They fled like frighted doos, man."

"O how deil, Tam, can that be true?
  The chase gaed frae the North, man;
I saw myself, they did pursue
  The horsemen back to Forth, man;
And at Dunblane, in my ain sight,
They took the brig wi' a' their might, bridge
And straught to Stirling winged their flight;
But, cursèd lot! the gates were shut;
And monie a huntit, poor red-coat,
  For fear amaist did swarf, man!" swoon

"My sister Kate cam up the gate road
  Wi' crowdie unto me, man; porridge
She swore she saw some rebels run
  Frae Perth unto Dundee, man:
Their left-hand general had nae skill,
The Angus lads had nae good-will
That day their neibors' blood to spill;
For fear, by foes, that they should lose
Their cogs o' brose — all crying pails of pottage
    woes;
  And so it goes, you see, man.

"They've lost some gallant gentlemen
  Amang the Highland clans, man;
I fear my Lord Panmure is slain,
  Or fallen in Whiggish hands, man.
Now wad ye sing this double fight,
Some fell for wrang, and some for right;
But monie bade the world guid-night;

Then ye may tell, how pell and mell,
By red claymores, and muskets' knell,
Wi' dying yell, the Tories fell,
And Whigs to hell did flee, man."

BLOOMING NELLY.

TUNE— *On a Bank of Flowers.*

ON a bank of flowers, in a summer-day,
For summer lightly drest,
The youthful, blooming Nelly lay,
With love and sleep opprest;
When Willie, wandering through the wood,
Who for her favour oft had sued,
He gazed, he wished, he feared, he blushed,
And trembled where he stood.

Her closèd eyes like weapons sheathed,
Were sealed in soft repose;
Her lip, still as she fragrant breathed,
It richer dyed the rose.
The springing lilies sweetly prest,
Wild-wanton, kissed her rival breast;
He gazed, he wished, he feared, he blushed,
His bosom ill at rest.

Her robes light waving in the breeze
  Her tender limbs embrace;
Her lovely form, her native ease,
  All harmony and grace:
Tumultuous tides his pulses roll,
  A faltering, ardent kiss he stole;
He gazed, he wished, he feared, he blushed,
  And sighed his very soul.

As flies the partridge from the brake
  On fear-inspirèd wings,
So Nelly starting, half awake,
  Away affrighted springs:
But Willie followed, as he should;
  He overtook her in the wood;
He vowed, he prayed, he found the maid
  Forgiving all and good.

MY HEART'S IN THE HIGHLANDS.

TUNE — *Faille na Miosg.*

In this song Burns caught up the single streak of poetry which existed in a well-known old stall song, entitled *The Strong Walls of Derry*, and which commences thus:

" The first day I landed, 'twas on Irish ground,
  The tidings came to me from fair Derry town,

That my love was married, and to my sad wo,
And I lost my first love by courting too slow."

After many stanzas of similar doggerel, the author breaks out, as under an inspiration, with the one fine verse, which Burns afterwards seized as a basis for his own beautiful ditty:

"My heart's in the Highlands, my heart is not here;
My heart's in the Highlands a-chasing the deer;
A-chasing the deer, and following the roe —
My heart's in the Highlands wherever I go."

My heart's in the Highlands, my heart is not here;
My heart's in the Highlands a-chasing the deer;
A-chasing the wild deer, and following the roe —
My heart's in the Highlands wherever I go.

Farewell to the Highlands, farewell to the North,
The birthplace of valour, the country of worth;
Wherever I wander, wherever I rove,
The hills of the Highlands for ever I love.

Farewell to the mountains high covered with snow;
Farewell to the straths and green valleys below;

Farewell to the forests and wild-hanging woods;
Farewell to the torrents and loud-pouring floods.

My heart's in the Highlands, my heart is not
here;
My heart's in the Highlands a-chasing the deer;
A-chasing the wild deer, and following the roe —
My heart's in the Highlands wherever I go.

THE BANKS OF NITH.

TUNE — *Robie donna Gorach.*

THE Thames flows proudly to the sea,
Where royal cities stately stand;
But sweeter flows the Nith, to me,
Where Cummins ance had high command.
When shall I see that honoured land,
That winding stream I love so dear!
Must wayward Fortune's adverse hand
For ever, ever keep me here?

How lovely, Nith, thy fruitful vales,
Where spreading hawthorns gaily bloom!
How sweetly wind thy sloping dales,
Where lambkins wanton through the broom!

Though wandering, now, must be my doom,
  Far from thy bonny banks and braes,
May there my latest hours consume,
  Amang the friends of early days!

MY HEART IS A-BREAKING, DEAR TITTIE!

My heart is a-breaking, dear tittie! sister
  Some counsel unto me come len',
To anger them a' is a pity,
  But what will I do wi' Tam Glen?

I'm thinking wi' sic a braw fellow
  In poortith I might make a fen'; poverty—shift
What care I in riches to wallow,
  If I maunna marry Tam Glen?

There's Lowrie, the Laird o' Drumeller,
  Guid-day to you, brute! he comes ben; in
He brags and he blaws o' his siller,
  But when will he dance like Tam Glen?

My minnie does constantly deave me, mother—deafen
  And bids me beware o' young men;

They flatter, she says, to deceive me,
  But wha can think sae o' Tam Glen?

My daddie says, gin I'll forsake him,
  He'll gie me guid hunder marks ten:
But if it's ordained I maun take him,
  O wha will I get but Tam Glen?

Yestreen at the valentines' dealing,
  My heart to my mou' gied a sten; bound
For thrice I drew ane without failing,
  And thrice it was written — Tam Glen.

The last Halloween I was waukin watching
  My droukit sark-sleeve, as ye ken; wet
His likeness cam' up the house staukin,
  And the very gray breeks o' Tam Glen!

Come counsel, dear tittie! don't tarry —
  I'll gie you my bonny black hen,
Gif ye will advise me to marry
  The lad I lo'e dearly — Tam Glen.

ELEGY ON PEG NICHOLSON,[1]

A DEAD MARE.

PEG NICHOLSON was a good bay mare,
  As ever trode on airn; iron
But now she's floating down the Nith,
  And past the mouth o' Cairn.

Peg Nicholson was a good bay mare,
  And rode through thick and thin;
But now she's floating down the Nith,
  And wanting even the skin.

Peg Nicholson was a good bay mare,
  And ance she bore a priest;
But now she's floating down the Nith,
  For Solway fish a feast.

Peg Nicholson was a good bay mare,
  And the priest he rode her sair;
And much oppressed and bruised she was,
  As priest-rid cattle are. — etc., etc.

Feb. 9, 1790.

[1] In burlesque allusion, it may be presumed, to the insane woman, Margaret Nicholson, who made an attempt to stab George III. with a knife, August, 1786.

WRITTEN TO A GENTLEMAN[1] WHO HAD SENT THE POET A NEWSPAPER,

AND OFFERED TO CONTINUE IT FREE OF EXPENSE.

KIND Sir, I've read your paper through,
And, faith, to me 'twas really new!
How guessed ye, sir, what maist I wanted?
This monie a day I've graned and gaunted, groaned yawned
To ken what French mischiéf was brewin',
Or what the drumlie Dutch were doin'; muddy
That vile doup-skelper, Emperor Joseph,
If Venus yet had got his nose off;
Or how the collieshangie works contention
Atween the Russians and the Turks;
Or if the Swede, before he halt,
Would play anither Charles the Twalt;[2]
If Denmark, anybody spak o't;
Or Poland, wha had now the tack o't: lease
How cut-throat Prussian blades were hingin';
How libbet Italy was singin': emasculated
If Spaniard, Portuguese, or Swiss,
Were sayin' or takin' aught amiss.

[1] Probably Mr. Peter Stuart, of the *Star* newspaper

[2] Gustavus III. had attracted considerable notice in 1789 by his vigorous measures against Russia, and the arrest of many of his nobility who disapproved of his measures.

Or how our merry lads at hame,
In Britain's court, kept up the game ;
How Royal George, the Lord leuk o'er him!
Was managing St. Stephen's quorum;
If sleekit Chatham Will was livin', smooth
Or glaikit Charlie got his nieve in; thoughtless—fist
How Daddie Burke the plea was cookin';
If Warren Hastings' neck was yeukin'; itching
How cesses, stents,[1] and fees were raxed, stretched
Or if bare —— yet were taxed;
The news o' princes, dukes, and earls,
Pimps, sharpers, bawds, and opera-girls;
If that daft buckie, Geordie Wales, mad
Was threshin' still at hizzies' tails; hussies
Or if he was grown oughtlins douser, any soberer
And no a perfect kintra cooser. stallion
A' this and mair I never heard of,
And but for you I might despaired of.
So gratefu', back your news I send you,
And pray, a' guid things may attend you! [2]

ELLISLAND, *Monday Morning*, 1790.

[1] Valuations of property for purposes of taxation.

[2] After all, from whatever cause, the gratuitous newspaper did not come very regularly, as appears from a subsequent note of remonstrance sent by the bard to head-quarters:

Dear Peter, dear Peter,
We poor sons of metre
Are often negleckit, ye ken;
For instance, your sheet, man,
(Though glad I'm to see't, man),
I get it no ae day in ten.—R. B.

SECOND EPISTLE TO MR. GRAHAM OF FINTRY.

The canvass for the Dumfries burghs had been proceeding with excessive vigor all this spring, and when the election at length took place in July, the agitation and fervor of the public mind in the district exceeded everything of the kind previously known. The influence of the Duke of Queensberry on the Whig side proved too much for the merits of excellent "Westerhall," and the dismissal of his Grace from the bedchamber was revenged on Pitt by the return of Captain Miller. In a spirited verse-epistle on the subject, addressed to his friend Mr. Graham, Burns still shows, under an affected impartiality, his Tory and even Cavalier leanings.

FINTRY, my stay in worldly strife,
Friend o' my Muse, friend o' my life,
    Are ye as idle's I am?
Come then, wi' uncouth, kintra fleg, country fling
O'er Pegasus I'll fling my leg,
    And ye shall see me try him.

I'll sing the zeal Drumlanrig[1] bears,
Who left the all-important cares
    Of princes and their darlings;

1 The Duke of Queensberry. Burns, for metre's sake, uses his Grace's second title.

And, bent on winning borough towns,
Came shaking hands wi' wabster loons, weaver
And kissing barefit carlins. women

Combustion through our boroughs rode,
Whistling his roaring pack abroad,
Of mad, unmuzzled lions;
As Queensberry buff and blue [1] unfurled,
And Westerha' and Hopetoun [2] hurled,
To every Whig defiance.

But Queensberry, cautious, left the war;
The unmannered dust might soil his star,
Besides, he hated bleeding;
But left behind him heroes bright,
Heroes in Cæsarean fight
Or Ciceronian pleading.

O for a throat like huge Mons-Meg,[3]
To muster o'er each ardent Whig
Beneath Drumlanrig's banners;
Heroes and heroines commix
All in the field of politics,
To win immortal honours.

1 The livery of Mr. Fox.

2 The Earl of Hopetoun.

3 A piece of ordnance of extraordinary structure and magnitude, founded in the reign of James IV. of Scotland, about the end of the fifteenth century, and which is still exhibited, though in an infirm state, in Edinburgh Castle. The diameter of the bore is twenty inches.

M'Murdo[1] and his lovely spouse
(The enamoured laurels kiss her brows)
Led on the loves and graces;
She won each gaping burgess' heart,
While he, all-conquering, played his part,
Among their wives and lasses.

Craigdarroch[2] led a light-armed corps;
Tropes, metaphors, and figures pour,
Like Hecla streaming thunder;
Glenriddel,[3] skilled in rusty coins,
Blew up each Tory's dark designs,
And bared the treason under.

In either wing two champions fought;
Redoubted Staig,[4] who set at nought
The wildest savage Tory,
And Welsh,[5] who ne'er yet flinched his ground,
High waved his magnum bonum round
With Cyclopean fury.

Miller[6] brought up the artillery ranks,
The many-pounders of the Banks,

1 The Duke's chamberlain, a friend of Burns.

2 Mr. Fergusson of Craigdarroch; the victor of the Whistle-contest.

3 Captain Riddel of Glenriddel.

4 Provost of Dumfries.

5 The sheriff of the county.

6 Mr. Miller of Dalswinton, father of the candidate. He had been a banker.

Resistless desolation;
While Maxwelton,[1] that baron bold,
Mid Lawson's port intrenched his hold,
And threatened worse damnation.

To these, what Tory hosts opposed,
With these, what Tory warriors closed,
Surpasses my descriving:
Squadrons extended long and large,
With furious speed rushed to the charge,
Like raging devils driving.

What verse can sing, what prose narrate,
The butcher deeds of bloody fate
Amid this mighty tulzie? conflict
Grim Horror grinned; pale Terror roared,
As Murther at his thrapple shored; throat—threatened
And hell mixt in the brulzie! broil

As Highland crags, by thunder cleft,
When lightnings fire the stormy lift, firmament
Hurl down wi' crashing rattle;
As flames amang a hundred woods;
As headlong foam a hundred floods;
Such is the rage of battle.

The stubborn Tories dare to die;
As soon the rooted oaks would fly,
Before th' approaching fellers;

[1] Sir Robert Lawrie, M. P. for the county.

The Whigs come on like Ocean's roar,
When all his wintry billows pour,
Against the Buchan Bullers.[1]

Lo, from the shades of Death's deep night,
Departed Whigs enjoy the fight,
And think on former daring!
The muffled murtherer of Charles [2]
The Magna-Charta flag unfurls,
All deadly gules its bearing.

Nor wanting ghosts of Tory fame;
Bold Scrimgeour[3] follows gallant Grahame,[4]
Auld Covenanters shiver;
Forgive, forgive, much-wronged Montrose!
While death and hell engulf thy foes,
Thou liv'st on high for ever!

Still o'er the field the combat burns;
The Tories, Whigs, give way by turns,
But Fate the word has spoken:

1 The "Bullers of Buchan" is an appellation given to a tremendous rocky recess on the Aberdeenshire coast, near Peterhead — having an opening to the sea, while the top is open. The sea, constantly raging in it, gives it the appearance of a pot or boiler, and hence the name.

2 The masked executioner of Charles I.

3 John, Earl of Dundee, noted for his zeal and sufferings in the cause of the Stuarts during the time of the Commonwealth.

4 The great Marquis of Montrose.

For woman's wit, or strength of man,
Alas! can do but what they can —
The Tory ranks are broken.

O that my e'en were flowing burns! brooks
My voice a lioness that mourns
Her darling cub's undoing!
That I might greet, that I might cry, weep
While Tories fall, while Tories fly,
From furious Whigs pursuing!

What Whig but wails the good Sir James —
Dear to his country by the names
Friend, Patron, Benefactor?
Not Pulteney's wealth can Pulteney save,
And Hopetoun falls, the generous, brave,
And Stuart bold as Hector![1]

Thou, Pitt, shall rue this overthrow,
And Thurlow growl a curse of wo,
And Melville melt in wailing!
Now Fox and Sheridan, rejoice!
And Burke shall sing: "O prince, arise!
Thy power is all-prevailing!"

For your poor friend, the Bard afar,
He hears, and only hears the war,
A cool spectator purely;

[1] Stuart of Hillside. *Closeburn MS.*

So when the storm the forest rends,
The robin in the hedge descends,
And sober chirps securely.

Additional verse in Closeburn MS. —

Now for my friends' and brothers' sakes,
And for my native Land o' Cakes,
I pray with holy fire —
Lord, send a rough-shod troop of hell
O'er all would Scotland buy or sell,
And grind them into mire!

ON CAPTAIN MATTHEW HENDERSON,

A GENTLEMAN WHO HELD THE PATENT FOR HIS HONOURS IMMEDIATELY FROM ALMIGHTY GOD.

"Should the poor be flattered?" — SHAKESPEARE.

But now his radiant course is run,
For Matthew's course was bright:
His soul was like the glorious sun,
A matchless, heavenly light!

Matthew Henderson appears to have been a "man about town," a kind-hearted, life-enjoying person, whose agreeable manners perhaps often made him welcome at tables better furnished than his own. He had been one of Burns's good-fellow friends during the time he spent in Edinburgh, and he appears as a subscriber for four copies of the second edition of our bard's poems — not, however, as *Captain* Matthew Henderson — but as "Matthew Henderson, Esq.," the "Captain" being, we understand, a mere pet-name for the man among his friends, adopted most likely from the position he held in some convivial society. Burns speaks of the poem as "a tribute to the memory of a man I loved much."

O DEATH! thou tyrant fell and bloody!
The meikle devil wi' a woodie — **rope**
Haurl thee hame to his black smiddie, — **smithy**
O'er hurcheon hides, — **hedgehog**
And like stockfish come o'er his studdie — **anvil**
Wi' thy auld sides!

He's gane! he's gane! he's frae us torn,
The ae best fellow e'er was born!
Thee, Matthew, Nature's sel' shall mourn
By wood and wild,
Where, haply, Pity strays forlorn,
Frae man exiled!

Ye hills! near neibors o' the starns, — **stars**
That proudly cock your cresting cairns!
Ye cliffs, the haunts of sailing yearns, — **eagles**
Where Echo slumbers!

Come join, ye Nature's sturdiest bairns,
My wailing numbers!

Mourn, ilka grove the cushat kens! wood-pigeon
Ye hazelly shaws and briery dens! groves
Ye burnies, wimplin' down your glens, meandering
Wi' toddlin' din, purling
Or foaming strang, wi' hasty stens, leaps
Frae lin to lin! waterfall

Mourn, little harebells o'er the lea!
Ye stately foxgloves fair to see!
Ye woodbines, hanging bonnilie,
In scented bowers!
Ye roses on your thorny tree,
The first o' flowers!

At dawn, when every grassy blade
Droops with a diamond at its head,
At even, when beans their fragrance shed,
I' th' rustling gale,
Ye maukins whiddin' through the glade, hares skipping
Come join my wail!

Mourn, ye wee songsters o' the wood!
Ye grouse that crap the heather bud!
Ye curlews calling through a clud! cloud
Ye whistling plover!

And mourn, ye whirring paitrick brood! —
He's gane for ever!

Mourn, sooty coots, and speckled teals!
Ye fisher herons, watching eels!
Ye duck and drake, wi' airy wheels
Circling the lake!
Ye bitterns, till the quagmire reels,
Rair for his sake! Roar

Mourn, clam'ring craiks at close o' day, landrails
'Mang fields o' flowering clover gay!
And when ye wing your annual way
Frae our cauld shore,
Tell thae far warlds, wha lies in clay
Wham we deplòre.

Ye houlets, frae your ivy bower, owls
In some auld tree or eldritch tower, frightful
What time the moon, wi' silent glower stare
Sets up her horn,
Wail through the dreary midnight hour
Till waukrife morn!

O rivers, forests, hills, and plains!
Oft have ye heard my canty strains: lively
But now, what else for me remains
But tales of wo?
And frae my e'en the drapping rains
Maun ever flow.

Mourn, Spring, thou darling of the year!
Ilk cowslip cup shall kep a tear: receive
Thou, Simmer, while each corny spear
Shoots up its head,
Thy gay, green, flowery tresses shear
For him that's dead!

Thou, Autumn, wi' thy yellow hair,
In grief thy sallow mantle tear!
Thou, Winter, hurling through the air
The roaring blast,
Wide o'er the naked world declare
The worth we've lost!

Mourn him, thou Sun, great source of light!
Mourn, empress of the silent night!
And you, ye twinkling starnies bright,
My Matthew mourn!
For through your orbs he's ta'en his flight,
Ne'er to return.

O Henderson! the man — the brother!
And art thou gone, and gone for ever?
And hast thou crossed that unknown river,
Life's dreary bound?
Like thee, where shall I find another,
The world around?

Go to your sculptured tombs ye great,
In a' the tinsel trash o' state!

But by thy honest turf I'll wait,
Thou man of worth,
And weep the ae best fellow's fate
E'er lay in earth !

THE EPITAPH.

Stop, passenger! — my story's brief,
And truth I shall relate, man;
I tell nae common tale o' grief —
For Matthew was a great man.

If thou uncommon merit hast,
Yet spurned at Fortune's door, man,
A look of pity hither cast —
For Matthew was a poor man.

If thou a noble sodger art,
That passest by this grave, man,
There moulders here a gallant heart —
For Matthew was a brave man.

If thou on men, their works and ways,
Canst throw uncommon light, man,
Here lies wha weel had won thy praise —
For Matthew was a bright man.

If thou at Friendship's sacred ca'
Wad life itself resign, man,
Thy sympathetic tear maun fa' —
For Matthew was a kind man.

If thou art stanch without a stain,
  Like the unchanging blue, man,
This was a kinsman o' thy ain —
  For Matthew was a true man.

If thou hast wit, and fun, and fire,
  And ne'er guid wine did fear, man,
This was thy billie, dam, and sire — fellow
  For Matthew was a queer man.

If ony whiggish whingin' sot, peevish
  To blame poor Matthew dare, man,
May dool and sorrow be his lot!
  For Matthew was a rare man.

TAM O' SHANTER.

A TALE.

"Of brownyis and of bogilis full is this buke."
GAWIN DOUGLAS.

According to the recital of Gilbert Burns, *Tam o' Shanter* originated thus: "When my father feued his little property near Alloway Kirk, the wall of the church-yard had gone to ruin, and cattle had free liberty of pasture in it. My father and two or three neighbours joined in an application to the town-council of Ayr, who were superiors of the adjoining land, for liberty to rebuild it, and raised by subscription a sum for enclosing this ancient cemetery with a wall: hence he came to consider it as his burial-place, and we learned that reverence for it people generally have for the burial-place of their ancestors. My brother was living in Ellisland, when Captain Grose, on his peregrinations through Scotland, stayed some time at Carse House in the neighbourhood, with Captain Robert Riddel of Glenriddel, a particular friend of my brother's. The antiquary and the poet were 'unco pack and thick thegither.' Robert requested of Captain Grose, when he should come to Ayrshire, that he would make a drawing of Alloway Kirk, as it was the burial-place of his father, where he himself had a sort of claim to lay down his bones when they should be no longer serviceable to him; and added, by way of encouragement, that it was the scene of many a good story of witches and apparitions, of which he knew the captain was very fond. The captain agreed to the request, provided the poet would furnish a witch-story, to be printed along with it. *Tam o' Shanter* was produced on this occasion, and was first published in *Grose's Antiquities of Scotland*."

"The poem," says Mr. Lockhart, "was the work of one day."

WHEN chapman billies leave the street, fellows
And drouthy neibors, neibors meet,
As market-days are wearing late,
And folk begin to tak the gate; road
While we sit bousing at the nappy,
And gettin' fou and unco happy,
We think na on the lang Scots miles,

The mosses, waters, slaps,[1] and stiles,
That lie between us and our hame,
Where sits our sulky sullen dame,
Gathering her brows like gathering storm,
Nursing her wrath to keep it warm.

This truth fand honest Tam o' Shanter,
As he frae Ayr ae night did canter,
(Auld Ayr, wham ne'er a town surpasses
For honest men and bonny lasses.)

O Tam! hadst thou but been sae wise,
As ta'en thy ain wife Kate's advice!
She tauld thee weel thou was a
skellum, reckless fellow
A blethering, blustering, drunken blellum;[2]
That frae November till October,
Ae market-day thou was na sober;
That ilka melder,[3] wi' the miller,
Thou sat as lang as thou had siller;
That every naig was ca'd a shoe on, driven
The smith and thee gat roaring fou on; drunk
That at the Lord's house, even on Sunday,
Thou drank wi' Kirkton Jean till Monday.[4]

[1] Break in a wall.

[2] An idle-talking fellow.

[3] "The quantity of meal ground at the mill at one time." — *Dr. Jamieson.*

[4] In Scotland, the village where a parish-church is situated is usually called the Kirkton. A certain Jean Kennedy, who kept a reputable public-house in the village of Kirkoswald, is here alluded to.

She prophesied that, late or soon,
Thou would be found deep drowned in Doon,
Or catched wi' warlocks in the mirk, darkness
By Alloway's auld haunted kirk.

Ah, gentle dames! it gars me greet, makes — weep
To think how monie counsels sweet,
How monie lengthened sage advices,
The husband frae the wife despises!

But to our tale: — Ae market-night,
Tam had got planted unco right,
Fast by an ingle, bleezing finely, fireplace
Wi' reaming swats, that drank divinely; foaming ale
And at his elbow, Souter Johnny, Cobbler
His ancient, trusty, drouthy crony;
Tam lo'ed him like a vera brither —
They had been fou for weeks thegither!

The night drave on wi' sangs and clatter, talk
And aye the ale was growing better;
The landlady and Tam grew gracious,
Wi' favours secret, sweet, and precious;
The Souter tauld his queerest stories,
The landlord's laugh was ready chorus;
The storm without might rair and rustle —
Tam didna mind the storm a whistle.

Care, mad to see a man sae happy,
E'en drowned himself amang the nappy!
As bees flee hame wi' lades o' treasure,

The minutes winged their way wi' pleasure:
Kings may be blest, but Tam was glorious,
O'er a' the ills o' life victorious.

But pleasures are like poppies spread, —
You seize the flower, its bloom is shed;
Or like the snowfall in the river, —
A moment white — then melts for ever;[1]
Or like the borealis race,
That flit ere you can point their place;
Or like the rainbow's lovely form,
Evanishing amid the storm.
Nae man can tether time or tide;
The hour approaches Tam maun ride:
That hour, o' night's black arch the keystane,
That dreary hour he mounts his beast in;
And sic a night he taks the road in
As ne'er poor sinner was abroad in.

The wind blew as 'twad blawn its last;
The rattling showers rose on the blast;
The speedy gleams the darkness swallowed;
Loud, deep, and lang the thunder bellowed:
That night, a child might understand,
The Deil had business on his hand.

Weel mounted on his gray mare, Meg,
(A better never lifted leg,)

[1] Candidior nivibus, tunc cum cecidere recentes,
In liquidas nondum quas mora vertit aquas.
Ovid, Amor. iii. 5, 11.

Tam skelpit on through dub and mire, slapped — puddle
Despising wind, and rain, and fire;
Whiles holding fast his guid blue bonnet,
Whiles crooning o'er some auld Scots sonnet; humming
Whiles glowering round wi' prudent cares, staring
Lest bogles catch him unawares: — goblins
Kirk-Alloway was drawing nigh,[1]
Where ghaists and houlets nightly cry. owlets

By this time he was cross the ford,
Where in the snaw the chapman smoored; smothered
And past the birks and meikle stane, birches
Where drunken Charlie brak's neck-bane;
And through the whins, and by the cairn, gorse
Where hunters fand the murdered bairn;
And near the thorn, aboon the well, above
Where Mungo's mither hanged hersel'.
Before him Doon pours all his floods;
The doubling storm roars through the woods;
The lightnings flash from pole to pole;
Near and more near the thunders roll;
When, glimmering through the groaning trees,

[1] "Alloway Kirk, with its little enclosed burial-ground, stands beside the road from Ayr to Maybole, about two miles from the former town. The church has long been roofless, but the walls are pretty well preserved, and it still retains its bell at the east end. Upon the whole, the spectator is struck with the idea that the witches must have had a rather narrow stage for the performance of their revels, as described in the poem." — *Chambers's Edinburgh Journal*, 1833.

Kirk-Alloway seemed in a bleeze;
Through ilka bore the beams were glancing, every hole
And loud resounded mirth and dancing.

Inspiring bold John Barleycorn,
What dangers thou canst make us scorn!
Wi' tippenny, we fear nae evil;
Wi' usquebae, we'll face the devil!—
The swats sae reamed in Tammie's noddle, ale—foamed
Fair play, he cared na deils a boddle.
But Maggie stood right sair astonished,
Till, by the heel and hand admonished,
She ventured forward on the light;
And, wow! Tam saw an unco sight!
Warlocks and witches in a dance;
Nae cotillon brent new frae France, bran
But hornpipes, jigs, strathspeys, and reels,
Put life and mettle in their heels.
A winnock-bunker in the east, window-seat
There sat auld Nick, in shape o' beast;
A towzie tyke, black, grim, and large, shaggy dog
To gie them music was his charge;
He screwed the pipes and gart them skirl, scream
Till roof and rafters a' did dirl. vibrate
Coffins stood round, like open presses,
That shawed the dead in their last dresses;
And by some devilish cantrip slight spell
Each in its cauld hand held a light:
By which heroic Tam was able

To note upon the haly table,
A murderer's banes in gibbet airns;
Twa span-lang, wee unchristened bairns;
A thief, new-cutted frae a rape, rope
Wi' his last gasp his gab did gape; mouth
Five tomahawks, wi' bluid red-rusted;
Five scimitars, wi' murder crusted;
A garter which a babe had strangled;
A knife, a father's throat had mangled,
Whom his ain son o' life bereft,—
The gray hairs yet stack to the heft:
Wi' mair o' horrible and awfu',
Which even to name wad be unlawfu'!

As Tammie glow'red, amazed and curious, stared
The mirth and fun grew fast and furious:
The piper loud and louder blew;
The dancers quick and quicker flew;
They reeled, they set, they crossed, they
    cleekit, linked
Till ilka carline swat and reekit, smoked
And coost her duddies to the wark, cast — clothes
And linket at it in her sark! fell to

Now Tam, O Tam! had thae been queans,
A' plump and strappin' in their teens;
Their sarks, instead o' creeshie flannen, greasy
Been snaw-white seventeen-hunder linen![1]
Thir breeks o' mine, my only pair, These

[1] "The manufacturer's term for a fine linen, woven in a reed of 1700 divisions." — *Cromek.*

That ance were plush, o' guid blue hair,
I wad hae gi'en them off my hurdies, loins
For ae blink o' the bonny burdies! wenches
But withered beldams, auld and droll,
Rigwoodie hags, wad spean a foal, Gaunt—wean
Louping and flinging on a cummock, short stick
I wonder didna turn thy stomach.

But Tam kenned what was what fu' brawlie;
There was ae winsome wench and walie, goodly
That night enlisted in the core,
(Lang after kenned on Carrick shore;
For monie a beast to dead she shot,
And perished monie a bonny boat,
And shook baith meikle corn and bear, barley
And kept the country-side in fear.)
Her cutty-sark, o' Paisley harn, short shift—huckaback
That while a lassie she had worn,
In longitude though sorely scanty,
It was her best, and she was vauntie.
Ah! little kenned thy reverend grannie
That sark she coft for her wee Nannie, bought
Wi' twa pund Scots ('twas a' her riches),
Wad ever graced a dance o' witches![1]

[1] A solitary-living woman, named Katie Steven, who dwelt at Laighpark, in the parish of Kirkoswald, and died there early in the present century, is thought to have been the personage represented under the character of Cutty-sark. She enjoyed the reputation of being a good fortune-teller, and was rather a favorite guest among her neighbors; yet with others, who knew her less, she was reputed a witch, addicted to those

But here my Muse her wing maun cour; stoop
Sic flights are far beyond her power;—
To sing how Nannie lap and flang
(A souple jad she was and strang),
And how Tam stood like ane bewitched,
And thought his very e'en enriched;
Even Satan glow'red and fidged fu' fain, fidgeted
And hotched and blew wi' might and jerked about
main:
Till first ae caper, syne anither,
Tam tint his reason a' thegither, lost
And roars out: "Weel done, Cutty-sark!"
And in an instant all was dark:
And scarcely had he Maggie rallied,
When out the hellish legion sallied.
As bees bizz out wi' angry fyke, buzz—fret
When plundering herds assail their byke; hive
As open pussie's mortal foes, the hare
When, pop! she starts before their nose;
As eager runs the market-crowd,
When "Catch the thief!" resounds aloud;
So Maggie runs, the witches follow,
Wi' monie an eldritch screech and hollow. frightful

Ah, Tam! ah, Tam! thou'll get thy fairin'! reward
In hell they'll roast thee like a herrin'!
In vain thy Kate awaits thy comin';

malevolent practices described in the poem. Neither her name nor her figure being appropriate (for she was a little woman), we confess we have doubts of this parallel.

Kate soon will be a woefu' woman!
Now, do thy speedy utmost, Meg,
And win the keystane[1] o' the brig;
There at them thou thy tail may toss;
A running-stream they darena cross!
But ere the keystane she could make,
The fient a tail she had to shake! deuce
For Nannie, far before the rest,
Hard upon noble Maggie prest,
And flew at Tam wi' furious ettle, — endeavor
But little wist she Maggie's mettle!
Ae spring brought off her master hale,
But left behind her ain gray tail:
The carline claught her by the rump, snatched at
And left poor Maggie scarce a stump.

Now, wha this tale o' truth shall read,
Ilk man and mother's son take heed!
Whene'er to drink you are inclined,
Or cutty-sarks run in your mind,
Think ye may buy the joys ower dear: —
Remember Tam o' Shanter's mare.

[1] It is a well-known fact that witches, or any evil spirits, have no power to follow a poor wight any further than the middle of the next running-stream. It may be proper likewise to mention to the benighted traveller, that when he falls in with *bogles*, whatever danger may be in his going forward, there is much more hazard in turning back. — *B.*

STANZAS ON THE BIRTH OF A POSTHUMOUS CHILD,

BORN UNDER PECULIAR CIRCUMSTANCES OF FAMILY DISTRESS.

Mrs. Dunlop had undergone a severe domestic affliction. Her daughter Susan had married a French gentleman named Henri, of good birth and fortune, and the young couple lived happily at Loudoun Castle, in Ayrshire, when (June 22, 1790) the gentleman sank under the effects of a severe cold, leaving his wife pregnant.

SWEET floweret, pledge o' meikle love,
And ward o' monie a prayer,
What heart o' stane wad thou na move,
Sae helpless, sweet, and fair!

November hirples o'er the lea — limps
Chill on thy lovely form;
And gane, alas! the sheltering tree
Should shield thee frae the storm.

May He who gives the rain to pour,
And wings the blast to blaw,
Protect thee frae the driving shower,
The bitter frost and snaw!

May He, the friend of wo and want,
  Who heals life's various stounds, pangs
Protect and guard the mother-plant,
  And heal her cruel wounds!

But late she flourished, rooted fast,
  Fair on the summer-morn;
Now, feebly bends she in the blast,
  Unsheltered and forlorn.

Blest be thy bloom, thou lovely gem,
  Unscathed by ruffian hand,
And from thee many a parent stem
  Arise to deck our land!

November, 1790.

ELEGY ON THE LATE MISS BURNET OF MONBODDO.

"I have these several months been hammering at an elegy on the amiable and accomplished Miss Burnet. I have got, and can get no further than the following fragment." — *Burns to Mr. Cunningham, 23d January*, 1791.

This beautiful creature, to whom Burns paid so

high a compliment in his *Address to Edinburgh*, had been carried off by consumption, 17th June, 1790.

LIFE ne'er exulted in so rich a prize
As Burnet, lovely from her native skies;
Nor envious Death so triumphed in a blow,
As that which laid the accomplished Burnet low.

Thy form and mind, sweet maid, can I forget?
In richest ore the brightest jewel set!
In thee, high Heaven above was truest shewn,
As by his noblest work the Godhead best is known.

In vain ye flaunt in summer's pride, ye groves;
Thou crystal streamlet with thy flowery shore,
Ye woodland choir that chant your idle loves,
Ye cease to charm — Eliza is no more!

Ye heathy wastes, immixed with reedy fens,
Ye mossy streams, with sedge and rushes stored,
Ye rugged cliffs, o'erhanging dreary glens,
To you I fly, ye with my soul accord.

Princes, whose cumbrous pride was all their worth,
Shall venal lays their pompous exit hail,
And thou, sweet excellence! forsake our earth,
And not a Muse in honest grief bewail?

We saw thee shine in youth and beauty's pride,
  And virtue's light, that beams beyond the
    spheres;
But, like the sun eclipsed at morning-tide,
  Thou left'st us darkling in a world of tears.

The parent's heart that nestled fond in thee,
  That heart how sunk, a prey to grief and
    care!
So decked the woodbine sweet yon aged tree;
  So from it ravished, leaves it bleak and bare.

LAMENT OF MARY QUEEN OF SCOTS ON THE APPROACH OF SPRING.

"The ballad on Queen Mary was begun while I was busy with Percy's *Reliques of English Poetry.*" — *Burns, February,* 1791.

Now Nature hangs her mantle green
  On every blooming tree,
And spreads her sheets o' daisies white
  Out o'er the grassy lea:
Now Phœbus cheers the crystal streams,

And glads the azure skies;
But nought can glad the weary wight
That fast in durance lies.

Now lav'rocks wake the merry morn,
Aloft on dewy wing;
The merle, in his noontide bower, blackbird
Makes woodland echoes ring;
The mavis wild, wi' monie a note, thrush
Sings drowsy day to rest;
In love and freedom they rejoice,
Wi' care nor thrall opprest.

Now blooms the lily by the bank,
The primrose down the brae;
The hawthorn's budding in the glen,
And milkwhite is the slae; sloe
The meanest hind in fair Scotland
May rove their sweets amang;
But I, the queen of a' Scotland,
Maun lie in prison strang!

I was the queen o' bonny France,
Where happy I hae been;
Fu' lightly rase I in the morn,
As blithe lay down at e'en:
And I'm the sovereign of Scotland,
And monie a traitor there;
Yet here I lie in foreign bands,
And never-ending care.

But as for thee, thou false woman!
My sister and my fae,
Grim vengeance yet shall whet a sword
That through thy soul shall gae!
The weeping blood in woman's breast
Was never known to thee;
Nor th' balm that draps on wounds of wo
Frae woman's pitying e'e.

My son! my son! may kinder stars
Upon thy fortune shine!
And may those pleasures gild thy reign,
That ne'er wad blink on mine! look kindly
God keep thee frae thy mother's faes,
Or turn their hearts to thee;
And where thou meet'st thy mother's friend,
Remember him for me!

O soon to me may summer suns
Nae mair light up the morn!
Nae mair to me the autumn winds
Wave o'er the yellow corn!
And in the narrow house o' death
Let winter round me rave;
And the next flowers that deck the spring
Bloom on my peaceful grave!

THERE'LL NEVER BE PEACE TILL JAMIE COMES HAME.

"You must know a beautiful Jacobite air, 'There'll never be peace till Jamie comes hame.' When political combustion ceases to be the object of princes and patriots, it then, you know, becomes the lawful prey of historians and poets." — *Burns to Mr. Cunningham, 12th March*, 1791.

By yon castle wa', at the close of the day,
I heard a man sing, though his head it was gray ;
And as he was singing, the tears fast down came, —
There'll never be peace till Jamie comes hame.
The church is in ruins, the state is in jars,
Delusions, oppressions, and murderous wars ;
We darena weel say't, though we ken wha's to blame, —
There'll never be peace till Jamie comes hame.

My seven braw sons for Jamie drew sword,
And now I greet round their green beds in the yerd: weep

It brak the sweet heart of my faithfu' auld
dame, —
There'll never be peace till Jamie comes hame.
Now life is a burden that bows me down,
Since I tint my bairns, and he tint his crown; lost
But till my last moments my words are the
same, —
There'll never be peace till Jamie comes hame!

LAMENT FOR JAMES, EARL OF GLENCAIRN.

At the close of January, Burns met a serious loss, both as respecting his fortunes and his feelings, in the death of his amiable patron James, Earl of Glencairn, who, after returning from a futile voyage to Lisbon in search of health, died at Falmouth, in the forty-second year of his age. The deep, earnest feeling of gratitude which Burns bore towards this nobleman is highly creditable to him. He put on mourning for the earl, and designed, if possible, to attend his funeral in Ayrshire. At a later time, he entered a permanent record of his gratitude in the annals of his family, by calling a son James Glencairn.

THE wind blew hollow frae the hills,
By fits the sun's departing beam

Looked on the fading yellow woods
  That wavèd o'er Lugar's winding stream:
Beneath a craigy steep, a bard,
  Laden with years and meikle pain,
In loud lament bewailed his lord,
  Whom death had all untimely ta'en.

He leaned him to an ancient aik,
  Whose trunk was mouldering down with years;
His locks were bleachèd white with time,
  His hoary cheek was wet wi' tears;
And as he touched his trembling harp,
  And as he tuned his doleful sang,
The winds, lamenting through their caves,
  To echo bore the notes alang:

"Ye scattered birds that faintly sing,
  The reliques of the vernal quire!
Ye woods that shed on a' the winds
  The honours of the agèd year!
A few short months, and glad and gay,
  Again ye'll charm the ear and e'e;
But nocht in all revolving time
  Can gladness bring again to me.

"I am a bending, agèd tree,
  That long has stood the wind and rain;
But now has come a cruel blast,
  And my last hold of earth is gane:

Nae leaf o' mine shall greet the spring,
  Nae simmer sun exalt my bloom;
But I maun lie before the storm,
  And ithers plant them in my room.

"I've seen sae monie changefu' years,
  On earth I am a stranger grown;
I wander in the ways of men,
  Alike unknowing and unknown;
Unheard, unpitied, unrelieved,
  I bear alane my lade o' care,
For silent, low, on beds of dust,
  Lie a' that would my sorrows share.

"And last (the sum of a' my griefs!)
  My noble master lies in clay;
The flower amang our barons bold,
  His country's pride, his country's stay!
In weary being now I pine,
  For a' the life of life is dead,
And hope has left my agèd ken,
  On forward wing for ever fled.

"Awake thy last sad voice, my harp!
  The voice of wo and wild despair;
Awake! resound thy latest lay —
  Then sleep in silence evermair!
And thou, my last, best, only friend,
  That fillest an untimely tomb,

Accept this tribute from the bard
  Thou brought from Fortune's mirkest gloom.

"In Poverty's low barren vale
  Thick mists, obscure, involved me round;
Though oft I turned the wistful eye,
  Nae ray of fame was to be found:
Thou found'st me, like the morning sun,
  That melts the fogs in limpid air;
The friendless bard and rustic song
  Became alike thy fostering care.

"O why has worth so short a date,
  While villains ripen gray with time?
Must thou, the noble, generous, great,
  Fall in bold manhood's hardy prime!
Why did I live to see that day?
  A day to me so full of wo!
O had I met the mortal shaft
  Which laid my benefactor low!

"The bridegroom may forget the bride,
  Was made his wedded wife yestreen; **last night**
The monarch may forget the crown
  That on his head an hour has been;
The mother may forget the child
  That smiles sae sweetly on her knee;
But I'll remember thee, Glencairn,
  And a' that thou hast done for me!"

LINES SENT TO SIR JOHN WHITEFOORD, BART. OF WHITEFOORD, WITH THE FOREGOING POEM.

Thou, who thy honour as thy God rever'st,
Who, save thy mind's reproach, nought earthly
fear'st,
To thee this votive-offering I impart,
The tearful tribute of a broken heart.
The friend thou valued'st, I the patron loved;
His worth, his honour, all the world approved:
We'll mourn till we too go as he has gone,
And tread the dreary path to that dark world
unknown.

THIRD EPISTLE TO MR. GRAHAM OF FINTRY.

From this time forth we are to see a chronic exasperation of spirit, affecting the life and conversation of the luckless bard. We get but slight and casual glimpses of the cause of all this acrimony; but I am assured that it would be a great mistake to attribute it wholly, or in any considerable part, to a mere jarring between the sensitive spirit of the poet and the rude contact of the worldly scene into which he was plunged. Burns did not want for a certain worldly wisdom and hardiness. His poetical powers had not in themselves exposed him to any serious evils. On the contrary, he was indebted to them for any advance in the social scene which he ever made, and even for such endowments of fortune as had befallen him. Neither was Burns so unworthily regarded by either high or low in his own day and place, as to have much occasion for complaint on that score. On the contrary, he had obtained the respectful regard of many of the very choicest men and women of his country. Whenever he appeared in aristocratic circles, his acknowledged genius, and the charms of his conversation, gave him a distinction not always readily yielded to mere wealth and rank. No: we have to look elsewhere for an explanation of the mystery. It seems to have mainly lain in the reckless violence of some of his passions, by the consequences of which he was every now and then exposed to humiliations galling to his pride. It was a refuge to his wounded feelings, to suppose that these passions were essentially connected with his poetical character.

[*Summer*, 1791.]

LATE crippled of an arm, and now a leg,
About to beg a pass for leave to beg;
Dull, listless, teased, dejected, and deprest
(Nature is adverse to a cripple's rest),

Will generous Graham list to his Poet's wail?
(It soothes poor Misery, hearkening to her tale)
And hear him curse the light he first surveyed,
And doubly curse the luckless rhyming trade?

Thou, Nature, partial Nature! I arraign;
Of thy caprice maternal I complain.
The lion and the bull thy care have found,
One shakes the forests, and one spurns the ground:
Thou giv'st the ass his hide, the snail his shell,
The envenomed wasp, victorious, guards his cell;
Thy minions, kings, defend, control, devour,
In all the omnipotence of rule and power;
Foxes and statesmen, subtle wiles insure:
The cit and polecat stink, and are secure;
Toads with their poison, doctors with their drug,
The priest and hedgehog in their robes are snug;
Ev'n silly woman has her warlike arts,
Her tongue and eyes, her dreaded spear and darts.—
But, oh! thou bitter stepmother and hard,
To thy poor, fenceless, naked child—the Bard!
A thing unteachable in world's skill,
And half an idiot, too, more helpless still;
No heels to bear him from the opening dun;
No claws to dig, his hated sight to shun;

No horns, but those by luckless Hymen worn,
And those, alas! not Amalthea's horn:
No nerves olfactory, Mammon's trusty cur,
Clad in rich Dulness' comfortable fur; —
In naked feeling, and in aching pride,
He bears the unbroken blast from every side;
Vampire booksellers drain him to the heart,
And scorpion critics cureless venom dart.

Critics! — appalled I venture on the name,
Those cut-throat bandits in the paths of fame;
Bloody dissectors, worse than ten Monroes![1]
He hacks to teach, they mangle to expose.

His heart by causeless wanton malice wrung,
By blockheads' daring into madness stung;
His well-won bays, than life itself more dear,
By miscreants torn, who ne'er one sprig must
wear;
Foiled, bleeding, tortured, in the unequal strife,
The hapless Poet flounders on through life;
Till fled each hope that once his bosom fired,
And fled each muse that glorious once inspired,
Low sunk in squalid, unprotected age,
Dead, even resentment, for his injured page,
He heeds or feels no more the ruthless critic's
rage!

[1] Alluding to the eminent anatomist, Professor Alexander Monro, of the Edinburgh University.

So, by some hedge, the generous steed deceased,
For half-starved snarling curs a dainty feast,
By toil and famine wore to skin and bone,
Lies senseless of each tugging bitch's son.
O Dulness! portion of the truly blest!
Calm sheltered haven of eternal rest!
Thy sons ne'er madden in the fierce extremes
Of Fortune's polar frost, or torrid beams.
If mantling high she fills the golden cup,
With sober selfish ease they sip it up:
Conscious the bounteous meed they well de-
serve,
They only wonder "some folks" do not starve.
The grave sage hern thus easy picks his frog,
And thinks the mallard a sad worthless dog.
When Disappointment snaps the clue of Hope,
And through disastrous night they darkling grope,
With deaf endurance sluggishly they bear,
And just conclude that "fools are fortune's care."
So, heavy, passive to the tempest's shocks,
Strong on the sign-post stands the stupid ox.
Not so the idle Muses' mad-cap train,
Not such the workings of their moon-struck
brain;
In equanimity they never dwell,
By turns in soaring heaven or vaulted hell.

I dread thee, Fate, relentless and severe,
With all a poet's, husband's, father's fear!
Already one strong hold of hope is lost—

Glencairn, the truly noble, lies in dust;
Fled, like the sun eclipsed as noon appears,
And left us darkling in a world of tears!
O hear my ardent, grateful, selfish prayer!—
Fintry, my other stay, long bless and spare!
Through a long life his hopes and wishes crown,
And bright in cloudless skies his sun go down!
May bliss domestic smooth his private path,
Give energy to life, and soothe his latest breath,
With many a filial tear circling the bed of death!

ADDRESS TO THE SHADE OF THOMSON,

ON CROWNING HIS BUST AT EDNAM, ROXBURGHSHIRE, WITH BAYS.

Written at the suggestion of the Earl of Buchan, for the inauguration of a temple built to Thomson on Ednam Hill.

While virgin Spring, by Eden's flood,
  Unfolds her tender mantle green,
Or pranks the sod in frolic mood,
  Or tunes Æolian strains between:

While Summer with a matron grace
  Retreats to Dryburgh's cooling shade,

Yet oft, delighted, stops to trace
  The progress of the spiky blade:

While Autumn, benefactor kind,
  By Tweed erects his agèd head,
And sees, with self-approving mind,
  Each creature on his bounty fed:

While maniac Winter rages o'er
  The hills whence classic Yarrow flows,
Rousing the turbid torrent's roar,
  Or sweeping, wild, a waste of snows:

So long, sweet Poet of the year!
  Shall bloom that wreath thou well hast won;
While Scotia, with exulting tear,
  Proclaims that Thomson was her son.[1]

[1] Burns, in looking into Collins for his verses to the memory of Thomson, had probably glanced at the same poet's exquisite *Ode to Evening*, for the three concluding verses are manifestly imitated in this Address:

"While Spring shall pour his showers, as oft he wont,
And bathe thy breathing tresses, meekest Eve,
    While Summer loves to sport
    Beneath thy lingering light:

"While sallow Autumn fills thy cup with leaves,
Or Winter, yelling through the troublous air,
    Affrights thy shrinking train,
    And rudely rends thy robes:

"So long, regardful of thy quiet rule,
Shall Fancy, Friendship, Science, smiling Peace,
    Thy gentlest influence own,
    And love thy favorite name!"

LOVELY DAVIES.

TUNE — *Miss Muir.*

Burns had become acquainted, probably at Friars' Carse, with a beautiful young Englishwoman, a relation of the Riddels, and also connected by the marriage of a sister with the noble family of Kenmure in the neighboring stewartry. Deborah Davies — for this was her name — was of small stature, but exquisitely handsome, and she possessed more than an average share of mental graces.[1] With his usual sensibility to female beauty, but especially that of a refined and educated woman, Burns became an idolater of Miss Davies, and the feelings which possessed him soon led to an effusion of both prose and verse. She was the subject of the two following songs.

O HOW shall I, unskilfu', try
The poet's occupation,

[1] "One day, while Burns was at Moffat" — thus writes Allan Cunningham — "the charming, lovely Davies rode past, accompanied by a lady tall and portly: on a friend asking the poet, why God made one lady so large, and Miss Davies so little, he replied in the words of the epigram:

"Ask why God made the gem so small,
And why so huge the granite?
Because God meant mankind should set
The higher value on it."

The tunefu' powers, in happy 'hours,
  That whisper inspiration?
Even they maun dare an effort mair
  Than aught they ever gave us,
Ere they rehearse, in equal verse,
  The charms o' lovely Davies.

Each eye it cheers, when she appears,
  Like Phœbus in the morning,
When past the shower, and every flower
  The garden is adorning.
As the wretch looks o'er Siberia's shore,
  When winter-bound the wave is,
Sae droops our heart when we maun part
  Frae charming, lovely Davies.

Her smile's a gift, frae 'boon the lift, above—sky
  That maks us mair than princes;
A sceptered hand, a king's command,
  Is in her darting glances:
The man in arms 'gainst female charms,
  Even he her willing slave is;
He hugs his chain, and owns the reign
  Of conquering, lovely Davies.

My Muse to dream of such a theme,
  Her feeble powers surrender;
The eagle's gaze alone surveys
  The sun's meridian splendour:

I wad in vain essay the strain,
  The deed too daring brave is;
I'll drop the lyre, and mute admire
  The charms o' lovely Davies.

THE BONNY WEE THING.

TUNE — *Bonny wee Thing.*

BONNY wee thing, cannie wee thing, "nice"
  Lovely wee thing, wert thou mine,
I wad wear thee in my bosom,
  Lest my jewel I should tine! lose
Wishfully I look and languish
  In that bonny face o' thine;
And my heart it stounds wi' anguish, aches
  Lest my wee thing be na mine.

Wit and grace, and love and beauty,
  In ae constellation shine;
To adore thee is my duty,
  Goddess o' this soul o' mine!
Bonny wee thing, cannie wee thing,
  Lovely wee thing, wert thou mine,
I wad wear thee in my bosom,
  Lest my jewel I should tine!

TO MR. MAXWELL, OF TERRAUGHTY, ON HIS BIRTHDAY.

The person addressed in these verses — John Maxwell, Esq., of Terraughty and Munches — was a leading public man in the county of Dumfries.

HEALTH to the Maxwells' veteran chief!
Health, aye unsoured by care or grief!
Inspired, I turned Fate's sybil leaf
This natal morn;
I see thy life is stuff o' prief, proof
Scarce quite half-worn.

This day thou metes threescore eleven,
And I can tell that bounteous Heaven
(The second-sight, ye ken, is given
To ilka Poet)
On thee a tack o' seven-times-seven lease
Will yet bestow it.

If envious buckies view wi' sorrow crabbed fellows
Thy lengthened days on this blest morrow,
May Desolation's lang-teethed harrow,
Nine miles an hour,

Rake them like Sodom and Gomorrah,
In brunstane stoure! brimstone dust

But for thy friends, and they are monie,
Baith honest men and lasses bonny,
May couthie fortune, kind and cannie, loving
In social glee,
Wi' mornings blithe, and e'enings funny,
Bless them and thee!

Fareweel, auld birkie! Lord be near ye, old boy
And then the deil he daurna steer ye: molest
Your friends aye love, your faes aye fear ye:
For me, shame fa' me,
If niest my heart I dinna wear ye, next
While BURNS they ca' me!

SONG OF DEATH.

AIR — *Oran an Aoig.*

Scene — A Field of Battle. — Time of the day, Evening. — The wounded and dying of the victorious army are supposed to join in the following song.

FAREWELL, thou fair day, thou green earth, and ye skies,
Now gay with the bright setting sun;

Farewell loves and friendships, ye dear tender ties,
Our race of existence is run!

Thou grim King of Terrors, thou life's gloomy foe!
Go frighten the coward and slave;
Go teach them to tremble, fell tyrant! but know
No terrors hast thou to the brave!

Thou strik'st the dull peasant — he sinks in the dark,
Nor saves e'en the wreck of a name;
Thou strik'st the young hero — a glorious mark!
He falls in the blaze of his fame!

In the field of proud honour, our swords in our hands,
Our king and our country to save,
While victory shines on life's last ebbing sands,
Oh! who would not die with the brave?

FOURTH EPISTLE TO MR. GRAHAM OF FINTRY.

The third Epistle to Mr. Graham, which has been assigned to the summer of 1791, expresses, though hintingly, the eager wishes of the poet for a better appointment in the Excise, and at length, by the kindness of that gentleman, it was obtained, towards the close of the year. He had expected, as we have seen, a supervisorship; but this was to remain a hope deferred. The arrangement was, that Burns should perform duty in Dumfries as an ordinary exciseman, and enjoy a salary of £70 per annum. This was an advance of £20 upon his Ellisland income, and as he did not now require to keep a horse, the advantage must be reckoned at a still higher sum. However this was, Burns considered himself as for the mean time independent of the farm. The income was indeed a small one, and it was something of a declension to be the common exciseman only; but hope at this time made up for all. He was led to expect an advance in the service, which, though increasing his toils, would put him comparatively at ease in his circumstances.

I CALL no goddess to inspire my strains;
A fabled Muse may suit a bard that feigns.

Friend of my life! my ardent spirit burns,
And all the tribute of my heart returns,
For boons accorded, goodness ever new,
The gift still dearer, as the giver you.

Thou orb of day! thou other paler light!
And all ye many sparkling stars of night!
If aught that giver from my mind efface,
If I that giver's bounty e'er disgrace,
Then roll to me, along your wandering spheres,
Only to number out a villain's years!

SWEET SENSIBILITY, HOW CHARMING.

We have but an obscure notice of a visit which Burns paid to Edinburgh in the November of 1791, being the last he ever made to that capital. Up to nearly this time, Mrs. M'Lehose had maintained the unforgiving distance which she assumed after his final union with Jean, notwithstanding his having sent her several exculpatory letters. She had lately written to him in a style which drew forth a letter in which Burns asks her opinion of the following verses.

SWEET Sensibility, how charming,
Thou, my friend, canst truly tell;

But how Distress with horrors arming,
  Thou, alas! hast known too well!

Fairest Flower, behold the lily,
  Blooming in the sunny ray;
Let the blast sweep o'er the valley,
  See it prostrate on the clay.

Hear the woodlark charm the forest,
  Telling o'er his little joys;
But, alas! a prey the surest
  To each pirate of the skies.

Dearly bought the hidden treasure
  Finer feelings can bestow;
Cords that vibrate sweetest pleasure
  Thrill the deepest notes of wo.[1]

[1] "I have sent in the verses *On Sensibility*, altered to

'Sensibility, how charming,
  Dearest Nancy, thou canst tell,' etc.,

to the editor of the *Scots Songs*, of which you have three volumes, to set to a most beautiful air — out of compliment to the first of women, my ever-beloved, my ever-sacred Clarinda." — *Burns to Mrs. M'Lehose.*

AE FOND KISS.

TUNE — *Rory Dall's Port.*

Clarinda had resolved, though with much hesitation, to accept an invitation from her heartless husband, and join him in Jamaica. In the softened feeling arising from the contemplation of such a movement, she relented so far towards Burns as to admit him to a visit. What one would give to know the particulars of the interview! It took place on the 6th of December. That it gave occasion to an effusion of passionate feeling, is strongly hinted in a letter of the poet written a twelvemonth after. We may also hesitate little in reading as a record of the scene a series of lyrics, one of which is amongst the most earnest expressions of intense feeling ever composed in verse.

AE fond kiss, and then we sever!
Ae fareweel, and then for ever!
Deep in heart-wrung tears I'll pledge thee,
Warring sighs and groans I'll wage thee.

Who shall say that Fortune grieves him,
While the star of Hope she leaves him?

Me, nae cheerful twinkle lights me;
Dark despair around benights me.

I'll ne'er blame my partial fancy;
Naething could resist my Nancy;
But to see her was to love her,
Love but her, and love for ever.

Had we never loved sae kindly,
Had we never loved sae blindly,
Never met, or never parted,
We had ne'er been broken-hearted!

Fare thee weel, thou first and fairest!
Fare thee weel, thou best and dearest!
Thine be ilka joy and treasure,
Peace, Enjoyment, Love, and Pleasure!

Ae fond kiss, and then we sever!
Ae fareweel, alas! for ever!
Deep in heart-wrung tears I'll pledge thee,
Warring sighs and groans I'll wage thee.

SONG.[1]

To an old Scots Tune.

BEHOLD the hour, the boat, arrive!
  My dearest Nancy, O fareweel!
Severed frae thee, can I survive,
  Frae thee whom I hae loved sae weel?

Endless and deep shall be my grief;
  Nae ray o' comfort shall I see,
But this most precious, dear belief,
  That thou wilt still remember me.

Alang the solitary shore,
  Where fleeting sea-fowl round me cry,
Across the rolling, dashing roar,
  I'll westward turn my wistful eye.

Happy, thou Indian grove, I'll say,
  Where now my Nancy's path shall be!
While through your sweets she holds her way,
  O tell me, does she muse on me?

[1] Another copy of this song is given further on, at p. 83 of vol. iii.

SONG.

To a charming plaintive Scots Air.

ANCE mair I hail thee, thou gloomy December!
Ance mair I hail thee wi' sorrow and care;
Sad was the parting thou mak'st me remember,
Parting wi' Nancy, oh, ne'er to meet mair!

Fond lovers' parting is sweet, painful pleasure,
Hope beaming mild on the soft parting hour;
But the dire feeling, oh, farewell for ever!
Anguish unmingled and agony pure!

Wild as the winter now tearing the forest,
Till the last leaf o' the summer is flown,
Such is the tempest has shaken my bosom,
Since my last hope and last comfort is gone!

Still as I hail thee, thou gloomy December,
Still shall I hail thee wi' sorrow and care;
For sad was the parting thou mak'st me remember,
Parting wi' Nancy, oh, ne'er to meet mair!

O MAY, THY MORN.

On the 25th of January, 1792, Mrs. M'Lehose wrote a friendly letter to Burns, bidding him farewell, in anticipation of her immediate departure for Jamaica. She says: "Seek God's favor, keep his commandments, be solicitous to prepare for a happy eternity. There, I trust, we will meet in never-ending bliss!" She sailed in February in that vessel, the *Roselle*, in which Burns had intended to leave his country a few years before.

One of the final meetings of Burns and Clarinda is believed to be the subject-matter of the following song, which, however, must be regarded as a poetical rather than historical recital.

O May, thy morn was ne'er so sweet
As the mirk night o' December,
For sparkling was the rosy wine,
And secret was the chamber:
And dear was she I darena name,
But I will aye remember;
And dear was she I darena name,
But I will aye remember.

And here's to them that like oursel'
Can push about the jorum;

And here's to them that wish us weel,
  May a' that's gude watch o'er them!
And here's to them we darena name,
  The dearest o' the quorum;
And here's to them we darena tell,
  The dearest o' the quorum.[1]

MY NANNIE'S AWA'.

In the course of the ensuing summer, while Mrs. M'Lehose was absent in the West Indies, the poet's feelings subsided into a comparative calm, and he then composed the following beautiful pastoral.

Now in her green mantle blithe Nature arrays,
And listens the lambkins that bleat o'er the
    braes,

[1] These lyrics could not have been written without an earnest, however temporary and transient, feeling on the part of the author; yet we conceive it would be a great mistake to accept them as a literal expression of the particular passion in which they originated, or a description of incidents to which that passion gave rise. We ought to make a considerable allowance for the extent to which the poet's mind is actuated by mere considerations of art and the desire of effect. In one there is a levity, and in others a tincture of *métier*, which are alike incompatible with our notions of this sentimental attachment. The *Ae Fond Kiss* appears in a different light. The tragic tale seems there concentrated in a wild gush of eloquence direct from the poet's heart.

While birds warble welcome in ilka green
shaw ; grove
But to me it's delightless — my Nannie's awa'.

The snawdrap and primrose our woodlands
adorn,
And violets bathe in the weet o' the morn ;
They pain my sad bosom, sae sweetly they blaw,
They mind me o' Nannie — and Nannie's awa'.

Thou laverock that springs frae the dews of the
lawn,
The shepherd to warn o' the gray-breaking
dawn ;
And thou mellow mavis that hails the night fa',
Give over for pity — my Nannie's awa'.

Come autumn, sae pensive, in yellow and gray,
And soothe me with tidings o' Nature's decay :
The dark dreary winter and wild driving snaw
Alane can delight me — now Nannie's awa' !

TO FERGUSSON.

It was probably about February, 1792, that Burns inscribed the following lines in a copy of *The World*, from which they have been copied.

ILL-FATED genius ! Heaven-taught Fergusson !

What heart that feels and will not yield a tear,
To think life's sun did set ere well begun
To shed its influence on thy bright career.
O why should truest worth and genius pine,
Beneath the iron grasp of Want and Wo,
While titled knaves and idiot greatness shine
In all the splendour Fortune can bestow!

THE DEIL'S AWA' WI' THE EXCISEMAN.

Tune — *The Looking-glass.*

" At that period [1792] a great deal of contraband traffic, chiefly from the Isle of Man, was going on along the coasts of Galloway and Ayrshire, and the whole of the revenue-officers from Gretna to Dumfries were placed under the orders of a superintendent residing in Annan, who exerted himself zealously in intercepting the descent of the smuggling vessels. On the 27th of February, a suspicious-looking brig was discovered in the Solway Firth, and Burns was one of the party whom the superintendent conducted to watch her motions. She got into shallow water the day afterwards, and the officers were enabled to discover that her crew were numerous, armed, and not likely to yield without a struggle. Lewars, a brother exciseman, an intimate friend of our poet, was accordingly sent to Dumfries for a guard of dragoons; the superintendent himself, Mr. Crawford, proceeded on a similar errand to Ecclefechan, and Burns was left with some men under his orders, to watch the brig, and prevent landing or escape. From the private journal of one of the excisemen — now in my hands — it appears that Burns manifested considerable impatience while thus occupied, being left for many hours in a wet salt-marsh, with a force which he knew to be inadequate to the purpose it was meant to fulfil. One of his comrades hearing him abuse his friend Lewars in particular, for being slow about his journey, the man answered that he also wished the devil had him for his pains, and that Burns in the mean time would do well to indite a song upon the sluggard. Burns said nothing; but after taking a few strides by himself among the reeds and shingle, rejoined his party, and chanted to them the well-known ditty." — LOCKHART. [See Appendix.]

THE deil cam fiddling through the town,
And danced awa' wi' the Exciseman,
And ilka wife cries: "Auld Mahoun,
I wish you luck o' the prize, man!"
The deil's awa', the deil's awa',
The deil's awa' wi' the Exciseman;
He's danced awa', he's danced awa',
He's danced awa' wi' the Exciseman!

"We'll mak our maut, we'll brew our drink,
We'll dance, and sing, and rejoice, man;
And monie braw thanks to the meikle black deil
That danced awa' wi' the Exciseman."

The deil's awa', the deil's awa',
The deil's awa' wi' the Exciseman;
He's danced awa', he's danced awa',
He's danced awa' wi' the Exciseman!

There's threesome reels, there's four- for three, etc.
some reels,
There's hornpipes and strathspeys, man;
But the ae best dance e'er cam to the land
Was—the deil's awa' wi' the Exciseman.
The deil's awa', the deil's awa',
The deil's awa' wi' the Exciseman;
He's danced awa', he's danced awa',
He's danced awa' wi' the Exciseman![1]

BONNY LESLEY.

"Such, so delighting and so pure, were the emotions of my soul on meeting the other day with Miss Lesley

[1] "Lewars arrived shortly after with his dragoons; and Burns, putting himself at their head, waded sword in hand to the brig, and was the first to board her. The crew lost heart, and submitted, though their numbers were greater than those of the assailing force. The vessel was condemned, and, with all her arms and stores, sold next day at Dumfries; upon which occasion, Burns, whose conduct had been highly commended, thought fit to purchase four carronades by way of trophy." —LOCKHART.

Baillie, your neighbour at M[ayfield]. Mr. B., with his two daughters, accompanied by Mr. H. of G., passing through Dumfries a few days ago, on their way to England, did me the honour of calling on me; on which I took my horse — though, God knows, I could ill spare the time — and accompanied them fourteen or fifteen miles, and dined and spent the day with them. 'Twas about nine, I think, when I left them, and riding home, I composed the following ballad, of which you will probably think you have a dear bargain, as it will cost you another groat of postage. You must know that there is an old ballad beginning with:

'My bonny Lizzie Baillie,
I'll rowe thee in my plaidie,' etc.

So I parodied it as follows, which is literally the first copy, 'unanointed, unannealed,' as Hamlet says." — *Burns to Mrs. Dunlop*, 22*d Aug.*, 1792.

O SAW ye bonny Lesley,
As she gaed owre the Border?
She's gane, like Alexander,
To spread her conquests further.

To see her is to love her,
And love but her for ever;
For nature made her what she is,
And never made anither!

Thou art a queen, fair Lesley,
Thy subjects we, before thee;

Thou art divine, fair Lesley,
  The hearts o' men adore thee.

The deil he couldna scaith thee, hurt
  Or aught that wad belang thee;
He'd look into thy bonny face,
  And say "I canna wrang thee!"

The powers aboon will tent thee; care for
  Misfortune sha' na steer thee; molest
Thou'rt like themselves sae lovely,
  That ill they'll ne'er let near thee.

Return again, fair Lesley,
  Return to Caledonie!
That we may brag we hae a lass
  There's nane again sae bonny.[1]

[1] Miss Lesley Baillie became Mrs. Cumming of Logie, and died in Edinburgh, July, 1843.

APPENDIX.

THE DEIL'S AWA' WI' THE EXCISEMAN.

There may be some flaw in the anecdote so far as this poem is concerned. At least it seems certain that Burns had other prompting for the composition besides his impatience with Lewars, for not only do we see that it is general in its application, but it also had a decided prototype in a poem written many years before, and with which Burns might well be acquainted.

" There lived, more than a century ago, a rhymer named Thomas Whittell, whose chief haunt was at East Shafto, in Northumberland, and who was buried at Hartburn in the same county, 19th April, 1736. His poems, as a ballad-book, have been extensively sold among the country people in the district in which he resided, and I have known them these sixty years. In 1815, they were published in a handsome form by Mr. William Robson, school-master of Morpeth, and from this copy I send you the following extract:—

" ' Did you not hear of a new-found dance,
That lately was devised on,
And how the Devil was tired out
By dancing with an Exciseman ?

"'He toes, he trips, he skips, he leaps,
As if he would bruise his thighs, man;
Sometimes the Devil made the better dance,
And sometimes the Exciseman.

"'The music was an enchanted pipe,
With which the piper plies on;
Betwixt them there was many a wipe, blow (?)
The Devil was in the Exciseman.

"'For sarabands, antics, minuets, jigs,
Or any dance you could devise on,
Although the Devil did dance them well,
He came not near the Exciseman.

"'They vaulted, leaped, and capers cut,
As if they would mount the skies, man;
The Devil to all his trumps was put,
To hold stick with the Exciseman.

"'The devil a dance e'er came from France,
But he had them before his eyes, man;
Had you beheld, I'd have been felled,
If you e'er saw one like the Exciseman.

"'It put the Devil beside his wits,
Whene'er he saw him rise, man;
There was the Devil upon Two Sticks
Betwixt him and the Exciseman.

"'They danced so long that from their snout
Sweat drops like dew from the skies, man;

The Devil ne'er had such a dancing-bout,
  As this was with the Exciseman.

"'At last the Devil began to faint,
  And saw he would lose the prize, man;
And, like a dull jade that had a taint,
  The other had cleared his eyes, man.

"'He stood like a mot,[1] and could not play toot,[2]
  He could neither vault nor rise, man;
But when the Devil was tired out,
  He carried away the Exciseman.

"'He that will take such a revel,
  For me shall have the prize, man;
'Tis equal to me, I like to be civil,
  Such company I despise, man.

"'For he that danceth with the Devil,
  I count him not a wise man;
His company is not fit for any,
  Except it be an Exciseman.'"

Extract from a Letter of Mr. Edward Riddle,
Greenwich, July, 1852.

It seems fair to conjecture, that Whittell had written this rough ballad at the time when the Excise was instituted by Sir Robert Walpole, 1733.

1 A mark for players at quoits. 2 Devil (?)

END OF VOL. II.

www.ingramcontent.com/pod-product-compliance
Lightning Source LLC
LaVergne TN
LVHW020227110826
845151LV00003B/842

* 9 7 8 1 4 2 5 5 3 2 5 6 7 *